Buckeye Believer

A 40-day
devotional playbook
for the Ohio State faithful

Del Duduit

BurnettYoung
BOOKS

Buckeye Believer By Duduit
Published by BY Books
P.O. Box 1
Clarklake, MI 49234

ISBN: 978-1-64071-018-4 (Print)
      978-1-64071-019-1 (Ebook)

Available in print and ebook from your local bookstore, online, or from the publisher at: www.BurnettYoungBooks.com

For more information on this book and the author, visit: www.DelDuduit.com

Brought to you by the creative team at Burnett Young Books:
Meaghan Burnett & Cyle Young

Library of Congress Cataloging-in-Publication Data
Duduit, Del
Buckeye Believer / Del Duduit

Printed in the United States of America

DEDICATION

This book is dedicated to my wife Angie, who has believed in me more than I have in myself at times. Thank you for the encouragement and help you have shown to me during this process. I remember the first Ohio State Buckeye football game we attended as a family. The boys were young, and we had a blast. The Scarlet and Gray won big that day, and the band had us on our feet before the kickoff. From that day forward, we were all Buckeye Believers. These are wonderful memories, and I pray this book will always hold a special bond in our marriage and life together. The best is yet to come. Go Bucks!

ACKNOWLEDGEMENTS

I want to thank the following people for their assistance in getting this book published:

- My wife, Angie, for your assistance in editing the initial manuscript and catching all of my silly goofs. Thank you for letting me disappear many evenings to write this book.

- My agent, Cyle Young, for your support and encouragement even though you played at the school up north. Thank you!! One day soon, I will focus on a devotional about the University of Michigan football program.

- My publisher, Meaghan Burnett, for not getting upset with me and letting me text you relentlessly during this process.

- My editor, Cristel Phelps, for your hard work and never-ending sarcasm.

- Jim Tressel, President of Youngstown State University and former OSU Football Coach. Thank you, Coach, for taking time out of your busy schedule to write the foreword for this devotional.

- Cindy Bell, Executive Assistant to Jim Tressel, and her staff for putting me in touch with President Tressel. You could have easily tossed my messages into the trash, but you delivered them, and great things happened. Thank you.

- God. Thank you for loving me.

FOREWORD

Ohio State Football is indeed rich in tradition. Many dynamic players and coaches come to mind: "Hopalong" Cassady, Archie Griffin, Woody Hayes, Eddie George, Chris Spielman and A.J. Hawk to Craig Krenzel, Ted Ginn Jr., Beanie Wells to Ezekiel Elliott and Urban Meyer.

I was blessed and honored to be a part of this great tradition by coaching the Buckeyes to a national title. Many exciting moments from that game come to mind.

I often think about Maurice Clarett taking back the ball right after the Miami interception. What a turning point. I recall Craig Krenzel diving into the end zone to tie the game and force the second overtime. And I think about Cie Grant blitzing the quarterback on the last play to secure the National Championship for Ohio State.

There's something special about the Scarlet and Gray and the Horseshoe. For players and fans, there is nothing on earth that compares.

Inside this book, Del Duduit brings many exciting OSU game moments back to life. He shows how we can take the lessons learned from some of the Buckeyes' best plays and apply them to our spiritual lives.

God allowed me to be a part of the great legacy that is Ohio State Football. For that I will always be grateful.

I hope you tackle each day with faith and accept the blessings the Lord has in store for you so you can be a Buckeye Believer!

Jim Tressel

CONTENTS

DAY 1

Today is Your Day of Salvation

January 3, 2003: Ohio State 31, Miami 24, 2OT National Championship

"In the time of my favor I heard you, and in the day of salvation I helped you. I tell you, now is the time of God's favor, now is the day of salvation."

—2 CORINTHIANS 6:2

Even though Ohio State entered the 2003 Bowl Championship Series (BCS) National Championship game ranked No. 2, they remained a long shot to win. The No. 1 ranked Miami Hurricanes were the heavy favorite.

The Miami offense was potent, and the defense was relentless. Prognosticators painted a bleak outlook for Ohio State. With those odds, why even play the game? No one gave the Buckeyes a realistic chance. The Hurricanes looked to repeat as national champs, while the Bucks hoped to win its first crown since 1970.

The game remained close throughout the night and ended tied in regulation. Quarterback Craig Krenzel bowled into the end zone for Ohio State and sent the game into a second overtime. No one expected this, except for the Scarlet and Gray. Running back Maurice Clarett bulled his way into the end zone in the second OT to put OSU ahead. Now the defense needed to do its job—rise and be heard.

Miami had the ball on fourth down and goal at the two-yard line. OSU linebacker Cie Grant blitzed from the corner. He gobbled up Miami quarterback Ken Dorsey and tossed him to the turf. Dorsey flung the ball in desperation, and it fluttered to the ground. Incomplete!

Grant's awareness of his surroundings allowed him to make the all-important last play, which saved both the game and secured the national title in Tempe, Arizona. After the contest, Grant was asked how he prepared for the final play. He did not hold back or hesitate. He said, "It's do or die time."

Like Cie Grant, are you ready for life's last play? Where will *you* spend eternity?

> *"And do this, understanding the present time: The hour has already come for you to wake up from your slumber, because our salvation is nearer now than when we first believed."*

> —ROMANS 13:11

4th and 1: For many of you reading this devotional, the Gospel of Jesus Christ has been preached to you for years, but very few can tell whether you are a Christian or not. All your friends and family pray for you to turn your life over to Him before it's too late. Or, maybe you have just recently heard about how the Lord can save you from your transgressions. In either case, you know what you must do. When you make a commitment to live a Christian life, it will be the best life-changing play you can make. You can ask God to save you and live a meaningful life—impactful and inspirational. Make the decision today—like Grant said, "It's do or die time."

Goal Line Stand: The Buckeyes made one of the most memorable goal line stands in football history. They dug in deep, claimed their turf, and came out victorious. If you are a non-believer and want to live for God, follow these three easy steps:

1. See your need for Jesus Christ. Without Him, life is hopeless. He is the reason any of us can experience real life today. You can be happy and live an abundant and complete existence because of Him.

2. Believe the Son of God died on a cross for your sins. He was placed in a borrowed tomb and rose from the grave three days later. He paid the debt for your sins so you could have life forever. Also, be comforted to know He will return one day to take His children home to be with Him throughout eternity.

3. Ask Him to come into your heart and life. Confess your sins to the Lord, and decide to defend your turf and claim spiritual victory.

Once you make the commitment, don't hesitate. Forge ahead and journey through a wonderful, productive life. Don't go back to your old ways, instead be excited for the promises God has in store for you. Defy the odds and be saved today. Make an all-out blitz for the Lord!

DAY 2

Bull Rush the Enemy

October 26, 2014: Ohio State 31, Penn State 24, 2 OT

"But as for you, be strong and do not give up, for your work will be rewarded."

—2 CHRONICLES 15:7

The No. 12 ranked Ohio State Buckeyes jumped out in front of Big Ten Conference foe Penn State 17-0 in State College, PA. OSU fans thought the game was in the bag. But the Nittany Lions had other plans and stormed back to send the game into double overtime.

Penn State faced a fourth and six from the OSU 21-yard line. They needed a first down or score to send the game into a third OT. With the game on the line, Buckeye defensive end Joey Bosa bull rushed the offensive line, shoved running back Akeel Lynch into quarterback Christian Hackenberg, and pulled Hackenberg to the ground.

The play sealed the 31-24 win for the Bucks in a tiresome game. Bosa said after the game he did not realize the play was a sack until everyone started to shout in celebration. His teammates jumped on top of him after he fell to the ground.

Have you ever been too weary to fight the devil? Let the Lord go to battle for you. It's wonderful to know you are on a victorious team.

"So do not fear, for I am with you; do not be dismayed, for I am your God. I will strengthen you and help you; I will uphold you with my righteous right hand."

—ISAIAH 41:10

4th and 1: Has life had an occasion to overwhelm you? Have you ever thought a situation has sent you into double overtime and the wrong choice might cost you the game? Perhaps you are tired of the fight with little results. Maybe you are certain the odds are too high to overcome. The enemy of your soul does his best to keep you feeling tired and discouraged.

Goal Line Stand: Now is the time to search and find the last ounce of strength you can muster to fight off the enemy who plots to destroy you. You think no one else will help you fight. You are by yourself. WRONG! The Lord Jesus Christ will *always* be there to help you fight your spiritual battles. You possess the playbook and are privy to the outcome of the game. Now, follow these suggestions:

1. *"Put on the full armor of God, so that you can take your stand against the devil's schemes."*

—EPHESIANS 6:11

Joey Bosa did not go into a game without his helmet and pads. Plus, he prepared his mind and body before each contest. As Christians, we need to prepare our spirit too. Review your game plan and pray to the Lord. Ask Him to show you what to do. Then put on the helmet of salvation with boldness, along with the belt of truth and the breastplate of righteousness.

2. <u>Take full aim.</u> Bosa did his job and rushed the line before it could stop him. He made the first point on contact, and his play saved the game. You, too, must execute God's plan and ask Him to take away any negative notions. Get off the line quick and bull rush the devil so he can't make the first strike on you.

3. <u>Trust God to deliver.</u> The Lord has promised to never put more on us than we can handle. Remember, there must be a glorious reward in store for you if you fight a spiritual battle. You may have a substantial lead in life, just like the Buckeyes had against Penn State. But out of nowhere, the lead can be wiped away. Be prepared for a spiritual marathon. Stay in shape, and read the Word of God each day—it's your playbook. Enhance your scouting report, and attend church on a regular basis. This is where you will receive encouragement and be prepped on any advances the devil will make against you. Now, talk to God. Prayer is your direct line to the coach's booth. He will always make the right call and put you in position to win the game.

Stay with God and take the fight to the enemy. Never sit around and be a stationary target. This is easy to hit. Be on the move with the Lord, and He will bull rush the forces of evil with you.

DAY 3

One Act Can Destroy a Reputation

December 28, 1978: Clemson 17, Ohio State 15

"My dear brothers and sisters, take note of this: Everyone should be quick to listen, slow to speak and slow to become angry—"

—JAMES 1:19

Many Ohio State fans may not remember the score. Some may not be able to recall the date. But what happened in the end will be a memory no one will forget.

The Buckeyes made a final drive to win the Gator Bowl in 1978 in Jacksonville, Florida. All they needed was a field goal to go ahead of Clemson. With less than two minutes left in the game, a pass by OSU quarterback Art Schlichter was intercepted by Charlie Bauman. Any hope of victory disappeared. Schlichter tackled Bauman out of bounds on the Buckeye sideline near the bench. Words were exchanged, and what happened next tainted a brilliant career.

Coach Woody Hayes, remembered for outbursts over the years, lost his temper and punched Bauman under the chin. Both teams emptied onto the field and had to be restrained. It took several minutes to break them apart.

More than 72,000 people attended the game, while untold thousands watched it on national television. Hayes lost control of his temper and piled up two unsportsmanlike conduct calls to add insult to defeat. After the game, the Buckeye coach did not address the media. No words were needed. His actions spoke loud and clear.

Athletic Director Hugh Hindman approached Hayes in the locker room after the game and gave the 65-year-old coach the chance to resign. Hayes refused the ultimatum and added his resignation would only make Hindman's job easier.

Hayes determined in his heart to go out with a blaze of embarrassment instead. After 28 years as the constant face of the mighty Ohio State Football program, Woody Hayes was fired within hours.

> *"Do not be quickly provoked in your spirit, for anger resides in the lap of fools."*
>
> —*ECCLESIASTES 7:9*

4th and 1: You may find yourself in a similar predicament. The goal you tried to reach is pulled away from you at the last moment. You become angry and frustrated. You intend to do what comes natural to the human flesh and lash out. Instead, you grit your teeth and want to strike an object—maybe even a person who wronged you at one time. Perhaps a person at work landed the promotion you felt you earned. Rage builds up in you when your colleague approaches. What do you do?

Goal Line Stand: You might be a little confused when you read Ephesians 4:26, because you see it says to be angry but don't sin. There were circumstances behind that verse. Anger can be justified at times in the Bible, but those are few and far between. For those who want to grow in their relationship with God and respond properly to an unpleasant circumstance, try these plays instead:

1. <u>Notice when your outbursts start, and seek God's grace at once.</u> Take control and admit there is a problem.

2. <u>Recite a Bible verse to calm you down.</u> Proverbs has some great examples. Find one or two, commit them to memory and use them in the time of distress.

3. <u>Pray.</u> Find guidance when you feel you might lose control of your emotions. Go to the Lord in prayer, ask Him to help you and He will.

4. <u>Think.</u> Take time to step back and examine the situation. This may not always be an option, but take advantage of the opportunity. Be slow to speak.

5. <u>Make sure you get enough sleep.</u> Take care of yourself, and make sure you get enough rest. If you are tired, you are more likely to maintain a short fuse.

6. <u>Exercise.</u> It's a great way to shift angry energy somewhere else.

In your Christian walk, you must learn how to control your temper. One act of anger can destroy a reputation and leave a negative memory. It doesn't matter if you are alone at home or on national TV, God notices your attitude and actions and doesn't like what He sees if those actions aren't part of His playbook for you. Don't let one negative incident damage your reputation. Instead, leave a positive legacy.

DAY 4

Praise, Praise and More Praise

January 1, 1953: Ohio State 10, Oregon 7

"Let everything that has breath praise the Lord."

—PSALM 150:6

The high-powered Buckeyes of Ohio State rolled into the Rose Bowl with hopes of a blowout over Oregon. But the Big Ten Conference champs found the Ducks to be tougher than they expected.

The Buckeye Nation anticipated a huge win for OSU. Needless to say, everyone who wore the Scarlet and Gray clinched their fists, sat on the edge of their seats and prayed a great deal as the game played out. Both teams scored in the first quarter, and the first half ended with a 7-7 tie. Neither squad put points on the board in the third period. Defense ruled the game. Ohio State's senior fullback Don Sutherin put the team ahead for good in the fourth quarter when he nailed a field goal for the 10-7 lead and eventual win.

A fullback who also kicks has to spend a lot of time on the practice field for both responsibilities. In 1958, the soccer style full-time kickers did not exist. All kickers used the head-on approach and style. Effective kickers must dedicate more time to perfect the skill and craft. In Sutherin's case, he practiced both the kick and the run. His work ethic paid off. Ohio

State kicked its way to Coach Woody Hayes' second Rose Bowl title.

Christians must also have the same work principles as Sutherin demonstrated. This comes in the form of praise to the Lord.

> *"Enter his gates with thanksgiving and his courts with praise; give thanks to him, and praise his name."*

—PSALM 100:4

4th and 1: Perhaps you are faced with a similar challenge. Sutherin had an entire team, university, and city on his shoulders. Everyone in the stadium watched to see if he could come through in the clutch. But that moment was not defined when he kicked the ball through the goal posts. The outcome resulted from practice and hours of dedication to his craft. The same holds true with a Christian. When you go through a tough situation, it will prepare you to be successful on life's journey. You cannot wait until the last minute to praise God and expect Him to deliver.

Goal Line Stand: Praise the Lord more today. Don't wait until the pressure is on and your life is on the line to call on the Lord. He might deliver you in a pinch. But if you make it a practice to praise and worship Him on a routine basis, you are much more prepared when a tough challenge arrives. Here are some fantastic ways to praise the Lord:

1. Praise Him by lifting your hands in honor to Jesus when you are in a church service. Don't worry about what others think. In fact, worship is contagious. You might inspire others to do the same thing.

2. <u>Praise Him with your mouth.</u> When you give a testimony in front of a congregation or in a Sunday school class, or even when talking with friends, this will make you a stronger Christian. Just a few words of praise can change an outlook.

3. <u>Praise Him with instruments.</u> If you have been blessed with musical talent, use it to glorify the Lord.

4. <u>Praise Him in song.</u> Again, if God has given you the ability to sing praise to Him, then do so. Being a good singer is not required, just having a desire to praise Him is all that is needed. You can also sing praises to Him if you are alone. He longs to hear you glorify His name.

5. <u>Praise Him with words.</u> Start a blog where you share the good news of Christ.

When you put your faith into action, you will become a stronger Christian. Nail the field goal and win the game. Keep your head down and focus on the ball. Fix your eyes on the Savior and follow through in your quest. Praise Him, praise Him, and praise Him some more—the practice is worth the extra point.

DAY 5

Make the Right Call

November 9, 2002: Ohio State 10, Purdue 6

"But blessed is the one who trusts in the Lord, whose confidence is in him. They will be like a tree planted by the water that sends out its roots by the stream. It does not fear when heat comes; its leaves are always green. It has no worries in a year of drought and never fails to bear fruit."

—JEREMIAH 17:7-8

Ohio State faced a fourth down and one. The ball laid on the Purdue 37-yard line with 1:40 to play. The entire season was on the line for the No. 3 ranked Buckeyes. An undefeated record and a chance to play for a national crown hung in the balance.

Then came the play.

Ohio State wide receiver Michael Jenkins broke open down the field. Quarterback Craig Krenzel stepped up in the pocket and floated a pass to Jenkins for the game-winning TD as the Bucks came from behind and defeated rival Purdue 10-6 in West Lafayette.

Jenkins was not the intended receiver. OSU Head Coach Jim Tressel planned for the pass to connect with the tight end, Ben Hartsock, for a much-needed first down. However, Krenzel, who majored in biochemistry, dissected the defense and noticed the safety out of position, which indicated Jenkins might be able to slip coverage. Dependable Hartsock became the decoy, and Krenzel saw Jenkins headed toward the goal line on the right side of the field. The pass hit Jenkins in stride for the score and the win.

Krenzel said later in an interview he had to make a split-second decision. "You don't have time to think, you just have to react." The choice to connect with Jenkins caught Purdue off guard. The score saved the game and the season for Ohio State. Bigger opportunities were to come for the Scarlet and Gray.

> *"For I know the plans I have for you," declares the LORD, "plans to prosper you and not harm you, plans to give you hope and a future."*
>
> —JEREMIAH 29:11

4th and 1: Perhaps you are faced with an important choice in life. What you decide might mean the difference in your overall happiness. Maybe you are given an option to take a promotion which would require you to move your family away from their friends. The decision might involve where to attend church or college. Choices. Everyone must make them. For every decision made, there is a consequence. Make your choice in life the right way.

Goal Line Stand: Craig Krenzel had a mere fraction of a second to make a decision that set the Bucks on a pathway to win the national title. Hopefully, you will have more time to make a life-changing choice. Here are some tips to consider when you must make tough calls in life:

1. <u>Pray.</u> This can be obvious but sometimes overlooked. You may be excited about a big event and say yes, because it's what you want. First have a conversation with the Lord about the circumstance. Ask if it's what *He* wants. Be careful not to talk yourself into the choice *you* desire.

2. <u>Gather the facts.</u> There are pros and cons to all decisions. Make a list of each and weigh the options. There are two sides to all stories. Proverbs 18 has some wonderful advice. Read this chapter before you go any further in your thought process.

3. <u>Make decisions at your pace.</u> If you are forced to choose, take that into consideration. Any positive choice can be planned out the right way. Be cautious about the once-in-a-lifetime opportunity. Put aside the fear you may never get that chance again. Don't act to obtain instant gratification. A decision could last a lifetime.

4. <u>Know your motivation.</u> This might be good and bad at the same time. If the decision is negative or made to hurt or embarrass someone, then it's easy. Say no. Be aware of what inspires you to make the selection. Make sure your motivation is pure.

5. <u>Look at all the caution signs.</u> If there are any doubts or red flags, they are there for a reason.

6. <u>Consider long-term results.</u> A decision made in seconds may have an impact for years. If you take your family away from a solid church to pursue a career, this might be selfish, but there may be positive results too. Make sure you take into account how this might affect your loved ones for years to come.

7. <u>Determine if the result of your action will glorify God.</u> Remember, we should do whatever is necessary to honor Him.

Be patient and pray for guidance. You never want to make a split-second choice which could hurt your reputation or chances for later success. Krenzel's action proved vital for his team, but Jenkins was not the intended target. An option call made at the last second proved successful. Life choices are not a game. Read the defense, check the playbook—your Bible, and make the right call.

DAY 6

Learn from the Loss

September 24, 1977: Oklahoma 29, Ohio State 28

"I have told you these things, so that in me you may have peace. In this world you will have trouble. But take heart! I have overcome the world."

—JOHN 16:33

Oklahoma shot out to a 20-0 lead in the first half in Columbus, and Ohio State had a fight on its hands. The Buckeyes battled back and responded with 28 unanswered points to take the lead. With less than two minutes to play, the Sooners needed a miracle, two of them in fact.

They scored a touchdown, but they were held at bay on the two-point conversion and trailed by a deuce.

The OSU defense prepared for the on-side kick. However, Uwe von Schamann squibbed the ball, and it hit a Buckeye first. Oklahoma recovered and now looked for an opportunity to win.

With three ticks left on the clock, von Schamann nailed a 41-yard field goal to give the Sooners a come-from-behind win. The 90,000 people at the Horseshoe were in shock. A wind blew behind him, and the snap came out perfect. The right conditions fell into place for Oklahoma to grab the win, while just the opposite happened for Ohio State.

The Bucks were stunned. They had battled back to take control of the game only to see it go by the way-side when the West Berlin native nailed the kick. They fought hard but still lost the game.

> *"So do not fear, for I am with you; do not be dismayed, for I am your God. I will strengthen you and help you; I will uphold you with my righteous right hand."*
>
> —ISAIAH 41:10

4th and 1: How do you deal with defeat? Ohio State did not opt to hang their heads and give up. Instead, they enjoyed a good season. The Buckeyes finished the year 9-3, which included a trip to the 1978 Sugar Bowl in New Orleans, LA. They lost the game 35-6 to Alabama. Perhaps you have worked hard for an achievement and it is pulled out from under you at the last moment. The devil uses discouragement as a tool to hinder a Christian from reaching full potential. He may use simple words from a friend to knock you down, or he may tackle your spirit with disappointments on the job.

Goal Line Stand: When you are faced with an unexpected loss, it may be easy to throw in the towel. But God does not desire that from you. He wants to see you stand and meet the challenge head on with a positive attitude. The key to spiritual success is to overcome obstacles and glorify God in the process. Here are some tips to beat discouragement:

1. Stay close to the Lord. The team discovered the game of life may be headed in the right direction, and victory can be in sight. But in an instant, a game-winning kick can feel like a punch in the gut. Find peace in the Lord, and

trust He has better plans for you around the corner. He wants to prepare you for a victorious future—you might encounter it sooner than you think.

2. <u>Stay alert.</u> Ohio State had the game won—all they needed to do was secure the on-side kick. Instead, they were caught off guard when von Schamann chose another option. Learn from "expecting the unexpected," and be open for other solutions God can bring. Be aware of all the tricks Satan may kick your way.

3. <u>Be honest with yourself.</u> Don't make excuses. Accept the loss and disappointment. Take responsibility. In the end, you are the one accountable for the overall results. A solid Christian can experience negative thoughts and emotions. Know this and cling to God for comfort. Believe the emotions are real, but also deal with them in a spiritual manner. Give them to the Lord.

4. <u>Be healthy.</u> When you are in shape, life in general appears better. This doesn't mean you have to be Charlie Atlas, but entertain a somewhat healthy lifestyle. Circumstances in life can drain a person's emotions at times. We need to be prepared in body, mind, and spirit to win the fight.

5. <u>Increase your time spent with God.</u> When going through extremely difficult pain, take a few more minutes each morning in devotions, or attend a Bible study with friends. Talk about your issues with those close to you, because it might do wonders to lift your spirits.

When you follow these suggestions, you can come back against an unexpected defeat and block Satan's kick the next time he threatens your victory.

DAY 7

Defend Your End Zone

Nov. 23, 2002: Ohio State 14, Michigan 9

"And my God will meet all your needs according to the riches of his glory in Christ Jesus."

—PHILIPPIANS 4:19

What a finish! One second remained on the clock. Michigan could see the end zone from 21 yards away. One more defensive stop was needed to preserve a perfect season and send the Buckeyes to the national championship game in the Fiesta Bowl.

Michigan quarterback John Navarre dropped in the pocket and fired his final prayer toward the end zone. More than 105,000 people watched in silence as the ball floated toward its target. Would the Wolverines put an end to Ohio State's bid for an undefeated season?

Buckeye defensive players Donnie Nickey, Mike Doss, and Will Allen made their stand. Allen snatched the pigskin out of the air for the interception to clinch the game. Ohio State ended the regular season 13-0 and co-Big Ten Champions and packed their bags for Phoenix to play for the national title.

The game was intense. There was no time to relax as the 9-2 Wolverines were either in the lead or within striking distance the entire game.

Ohio State's freshman sensation running back Maurice Clarett returned from an injury and put the Bucks ahead 7-3 early in the first quarter. Three first-half field goals gave the team up north a 9-7 lead before the half.

Neither team scored in the third stanza. However, OSU signal caller Craig Krenzel orchestrated the go-ahead drive from the Michigan 42-yard line with just over eight minutes to go in the game. It culminated when Krenzel optioned to Maurice Hall for the TD from two yards out. From there, the Buckeye defense secured the win and kept the perfect season intact.

Now was the time to stand and deliver. If the defense had not risen to the occasion, defeat would have been certain. No perfect season and no hopes for a national championship.

> *"Shake off your dust; rise up, sit enthroned, Jerusalem. Free yourself from the chains on your neck, Daughter Zion, now a captive."*
>
> —ISAIAH 52:2

4th and 1: As a Christian, you are always a target of the devil. His sole purpose is to destroy God's children. He wants to defeat you and tear your family apart. If he can accomplish that mission, he will win the game and knock you out of contention for your title crown. He doesn't play fair. He uses lies and your past to get you to fumble.

Goal Line Stand: Christians face spiritual battles. Some may appear more dramatic than others. In your day-to-day walk, be vigilant because an active demon wants to destroy you and your family. You might not realize it most times, but these forces are real. A good coach will know his opponent. You, too, must be familiar with your adversary. How can you battle your enemy if you don't understand who or what he is? An effective coach will prepare his team with scouting reports and study every move the opposition makes on certain plays. You have to do the same. You must be aware how and when the rival may try to strike a blow. In today's rapid lifestyle, it might be easy to lose focus and not realize the game plan of the enemy. The world is full of distractions to keep your mind off spiritual matters. How can you prepare for Satan's next attack? Follow your scouting report. Educate yourself on the devil's modus operandi:

1. He is a deceiver.

2. He is a liar.

3. He is the accuser.

4. He steals.

5. He disguises himself.

6. He is our adversary.

7. He is a tempter.

8. He is sneaky.

9. He hinders and binds.

10. He destroys.

Know your enemy inside and out. Be aware when he plans to drop back and make the final pass to win the game and ruin your life. If you are on to his tactics, your defenses will rise to the occasion and win the game with no time left to play. What a finish!

DAY 8

Live for Each Day

November 19, 1994: Ohio State 22, Michigan 6

"The Lord has done it this very day; let us rejoice today and be glad."

—PSALM 118:24

Ohio State needed someone to step up and make a big play. Rival Michigan trailed 12-6, but the Wolverines seized momentum after consecutive field goals pulled them to within a touchdown. They were in prime position to get even closer. Michigan wide receiver Amani Toomer was free in the end zone, but quarterback Todd Collins could not connect with the target in bounds.

Ohio State corner back Marlon Kerner had been beaten on the play. But he got off the hook when Collin's pass took Toomer out of bounds. Kerner said he dodged a bullet. He felt pressure to step up and make a dynamic play.

Michigan opted for a field goal. A three-pointer would cut the deficit to three.

Kerner responded to his earlier blunder and swung around the end to block Remy Hamilton's field-goal attempt. That play later resulted in an Ohio State field goal and boosted the lead, 15-6. The blocked kick shifted the momentum in the game. Later, Ohio State's nose tackle Luke Fickell intercepted a pass from Collins to thwart another possible score inside the red zone.

Both Kerner and Fickell rose to the occasion and made defensive plays to help Ohio State secure a 22-6 win over Michigan at the Horseshoe in front of 94,000 people. They lived in the moment, made the play, and delivered for their team.

"Therefore do not worry about tomorrow, for tomorrow will worry about itself. Each day has enough trouble of its own."

—MATTHEW 6:34

4th and 1: Do you put off or delay what you can do for God? Do you long to make an impactful play for the Lord? Why do you procrastinate? Do the miraculous today! The whole world doesn't have to notice. Make this the day you make your big play.

Goal Line Stand: Okay. You shared views and thoughts and want to put them into action, but you have an adversary. The opponent stands ready to score. It's time to deliver and show up for your team. Here are some suggestions to help your squad win the game:

1. Volunteer for a local charity. Do your research and make a solid commitment to give your time at least once a month if not more.

2. Become a Big Brother or Big Sister. When you mentor a child, you participate in a worthwhile cause. Be the example these children desire.

3. Offer to do outdoor maintenance for a senior citizen or an older couple. Do not take compensation from them—

except maybe if it's a glass of lemonade or water. Do a better job than you would do for your own property.

4. Become involved in youth sports. Shine a light to young children in athletics, and be a positive role model to parents.

5. Offer to clean or pick up trash after a high school event, like a football game. There is no glory in this action, but it will make you feel good when you are finished.

6. Make regular visits to people you know in the local hospital or hospice unit. When you give your time and let people see you care, it means a lot to those who are in need.

7. Start a Christian blog as a ministry. This is one you can do right now, but post a goal and stay committed to it.

8. Organize your own garage sale, and dedicate the money raised to a local charity.

9. Establish a Bible study.

10. Get involved in local, state, or national politics. Christians, now more than ever, must let their voices be heard. Show them there are people who will stand for the right cause.

Make your dynamic play now. You have waited long enough and almost got burned like Marlon Kerner. He responded and delivered for the Buckeyes. Make your stand and block the devil's kick. If you sit back and don't act, you will fall into his terrible game plan for your life.

DAY 9

Battle the Elements

October 30, 1993: Ohio State 24, Penn State 6

"As they sailed, he fell asleep. A squall came down on the lake, so that the boat was being swamped, and they were in great danger."

—LUKE 8:23

Ranked No. 3 Ohio State played host to No. 12 Penn State the day before Halloween. Weather conditions were horrible. Snow mixed with rain and 33-degree temperatures at the Horseshoe in Columbus kept the crowd frozen.

The Buckeyes jumped to a 17-6 halftime lead and controlled the game to hold on for the Big Ten Conference win. The victory was sizable for OSU, because it put them at 8-0 and in prime position for a trip to the Rose Bowl.

Tailback Raymond Harris had a career-high day as he toted the pigskin 32 times for 151 yards. The game plan for snow meant a steady stream of run-it-down-your-throat style of football, since nasty weather conditions made it hard to pass. The Nittany Lions could not handle the offensive line while the defensive front wreaked havoc with Penn State signal caller Kerry Collins.

Ohio State overcame bad weather conditions, while their opponent did not. The Bucks played solid football, while Penn State could not adapt to the elements.

Are you in a storm?

> *"The disciples went and woke him, saying, 'Master, Master, we're going to drown!' He got up and rebuked the wind and the raging waters; the storm subsided, and all was calm. 'Where is your faith?' He asked his disciples. In fear and amazement they asked one another, 'Who is this? He commands even the winds and the water, and they obey him.'"*

—LUKE 8:24-25

4th and 1: Do bad conditions make it impossible for you to perform? Life can be sunny one day and a blizzard the next. Out of nowhere, the storms of life can leave you stranded with no sense of direction. The gale can take shapes. Maybe it's a horrible personal struggle or the loss of a job. Perhaps someone close to you passed away with no warning, or your child stares danger in the face. An unresolved life struggle can linger and make you feel helpless. There are two choices. Either give up and let the elements take their toll on you, or develop a plan to maneuver through the whirlwind.

Goal Line Stand: The main objective in weathering life's storms is to be prepared for them to happen. Struggles come when you are caught off guard. If you are equipped to seek shelter when uproars occur, you will sustain less damage than others who are not ready. Here are some ways to steady yourself for the unpredicted rages of life:

1. <u>Stay in the Word of God—the Bible.</u> Protect your quiet time each day with the Lord. You will become closer to Him through the struggles, and your personal relationship with Him will grow stronger.

2. <u>Memorize scripture.</u> Find verses that give you comfort and commit them to memory.

3. <u>Praise God for all you have.</u> The Lord enjoys it when we recognize and honor Him. Practice praising Him when all is calm so you can do the same when a storm approaches.

4. <u>Pray often.</u> You hold conversations with your spouse, children, and friends. Talking with the Lord is just as important. Make it a point to fill an entire prayer with gratitude for what He has done without asking Him for any requests. When you talk to your Father in Heaven on a regular schedule, it will help you to depend on Him in times when you need Him the most. He will always be there for you.

When the conditions are not perfect, it may be difficult to hunker down and ride out the storm. Sometimes it might mean you take a direct hit and suffer damage. However, when you read the Bible on a regular basis, combined with prayer and praise, you will be able to withstand the blusters of life better and live to see a brighter day. Be prepared and demonstrate an effective ground game, proving your readiness to cope with the struggles of life.

DAY 10

Wait on the Lord

January 2, 1984: Ohio State 28, Pittsburgh 23

"Wait for the Lord; be strong and take heart and wait for the Lord."

—PSALM 27:14

Thad Jemison had waited for this moment for a long time. The 6'2" senior from Cincinnati spent a lot of time on the Buckeye bench. He was frustrated yet remained hopeful his big break would come.

Boy, did it ever. In his last game to wear the Scarlet and Gray, Jemison ended his career in storybook fashion. With 39 seconds left on the clock, he pulled in a pass from Mike Tomczak to give the Buckeyes a dramatic 28-23 victory over Pitt in the Fiesta Bowl at Sun Devil Stadium in Tempe, Arizona.

Before his heroics, the Bucks were in position to lose the game to Pitt. The Panthers took the lead on a field goal with 2:30 left to play. That's all the time Tomczak needed to march the offense down to the Pitt 39-yard line.

Jemison's third TD of the season came at a crucial time for both him and OSU. The game-winning reception capped off a wonderful performance. He hauled in eight catches for 131 yards, which tied a Fiesta Bowl record.

Although he desperately wanted to play every second of his career, he waited for the call from the coach. He waited for his time to shine. He was the key that opened the doors to the title.

> *"I wait for the Lord, my whole being waits, and in his word I put my hope."*

> —PSALM 130:5

4th and 1: If you are like me, I struggle to wait and lack patience at times. In fact, the entire population has issues with this. We live in an on-demand society. We want it now. People can't wait to get the latest version of the iPhone before it even comes out. Patience is hard to have in today's world. However, there are times when it must be demonstrated. When you try to force an outcome, it often backfires and might lead to unpleasant results. Had Jemison grown impatient and transferred to another school, he would have missed out on a memory which lives forever in the hearts of the Buckeye faithful. He might have seen the field more elsewhere, but he may not have lived a moment like the one he experienced at the Fiesta Bowl. Often, we can't see the overall picture, but we can demonstrate trust in the Lord when He tells us to be still and wait.

Goal Line Stand: Here are some tips to be patient and let God take control:

1. Your predicament is not too difficult for the Creator of the universe. God will not give you more than you can handle. If you don't hear back from a company regarding a job interview, just wait. It's difficult to be unemployed

and understandable to want the job—now. But trust the Lord has your circumstances under control, and the answer will come in His time.

2. <u>Concentrate on the positive outcome that will emerge from a time of waiting.</u> Make good use of the time you are in limbo. Grow deeper in the Word and improve your prayer life. Don't sit around and worry. Use the extra down time to do something productive. Substitute the stress with action. Focus your attention on a charity or participate in an after-school program. Find ways to help others while you wait.

3. <u>Anticipate and find opportunities to glorify Him.</u> In fact, honor Him all the time—not just when you want something wonderful to happen. Don't praise God so He will return the favor and answer your prayer. Praise Him because He is holy. Always give God the glory. Expect God to deliver, but be ready to accept His plan for your life.

Jemison waited on his opportunity and made the most out of a fantastic moment. Your time will come. It might not be when you think, but it will present itself when you need it more than ever. Be ready. Practice. Read your Bible, pray, and go to church. At the moment you least expect it, the ball will head your way for the touchdown to win the game.

DAY 11

Run Like the Wind

November 15, 2014: Ohio State 31, Minnesota 24

"He mounted the cherubim and flew; he soared on the wings of the wind."

—2 SAMUEL 22:11

The No. 7 ranked Ohio State Buckeyes marched into Minneapolis and expected to increase their odds to reach the BCS Championship game. They did not anticipate below freezing temperatures along with snow and a strong wind.

Target Field buzzed with excitement on Senior Day. At the start of the first quarter, Ohio State quarterback J.T. Barrett took the keeper up the middle and outran several defenders 86 yards for the touchdown. He set the tone, and the Bucks held on for the 31-24 win. The play was what OSU needed to combat the crowd, the snow, and the wind.

"Suddenly a sound like the blowing of a violent wind came from heaven and filled the whole house where they were sitting."

—ACTS 2:2

4th and 1: Imagine you are in a church service or a revival, and you can feel the move of God throughout the sanctuary. People are being blessed by the Spirit and at the altar in prayer.

Suddenly, a person stands and gives a strange testimony that knocks the wind out of the service and quenches the Holy Spirit. We have all seen this happen, and there are many ways to drive away the presence of the Lord.

The Holy Ghost lights a fire of joy within us as children of the King. He longs to manifest Himself through us. When we lift our hands in praise to Him, He fills us with His peace. Always be open to let Him move through you, and obey the Lord's commands. For if you suppress the Spirit and do not allow yourself to be used, it may vanish. Let God express Himself through you, and do not try to dictate how it is demonstrated. Be willing to be a blessing to others and bring unity to the body of Christ.

Goal Line Stand: No one wants to be the reason the wind leaves your service. As children of Christ, we desire to praise Him and do our part to uplift and show others the love He has for us. But there are times when you could grieve the Holy Spirit, and here are some examples:

1. When you are bitter. There is no place in a Christian's heart for this. When bitterness dwells in your heart, you will feel alone. No one wants to be around a negative person. Let it go, and live the life God has in store for you.

2. When you don't forgive others. The Bible tells us in a distinct manner to forgive people, even when they are the ones in the wrong. Give it to God, and worship Him. He will take care of the problem.

3. When you are angry. If you harbor resentment, you cannot be an effective witness to others. Anger may be justified at times, but those are few and far between.

Realize the difference between when anger is necessary and when it is pointless and unwarranted. Most times your heated response will not glorify God.

4. <u>When you steal.</u> You cannot be an effective representation of His goodness if you take what is not yours. From the moment you break a commandment, you quench the Holy Spirit in your life.

5. <u>When you use derogatory language.</u> This sets the tone for a negative witness. Use upbeat language and bring glory to the Lord. Don't even use it when you are alone. When you allow bad language in your thoughts, it will come out when you least expect it.

6. <u>When you don't tell the truth.</u> Avoid a lie, which can lead people down a wrong path, because you could become lost and might not find your way back. Once you start, it is hard to quit. Also, one of God's attributes is truth. If you are not truthful, then you are not able to be as close to Him as you desire.

7. <u>When you live like the world</u>. You are called to be set apart and establish yourself as a child of the King. You cannot wallow in a pig pen without getting dirty. Watch where you go and how you behave. The world expects more from you and observes your walk.

8. <u>When you are rude or arrogant.</u> Instead be humble and show gratitude.

9. <u>When you want to be the center of attention.</u> The Lord should be seen, not you. Shine the light on Him.

10. <u>When you are immoral.</u> You need to live by His rules and be an upright citizen of the kingdom of Heaven. If you sense the need to perform an unrighteous act in pri-

vate or feel the need to hide whatever it is you are doing, remember the Lord still sees your actions.

Avoid these to keep the Holy Spirit in your life. Welcome and revere the presence of God. Take comfort when you experience His gentle breeze blow by, and you'll know it's the Lord.

DAY 12

Always Be Prepared

November 22, 1969: Michigan 21, Ohio State 12

"Therefore keep watch, because you do not know on what day your Lord will come. But understand this: If the owner of the house had known at what time of night the thief was coming, he would have kept watch and would not have let his house be broken into."

—MATTHEW 24:42-43

The mighty No. 1 ranked Ohio State Buckeyes marched into The Big House in late November with plans to play for a Big Ten crown and a national title. All they needed to do was knock off unranked Michigan and secure the invitation to the Rose Bowl. Easy enough, right?

The Wolverines came prepared with a game plan to stun the Bucks and end the OSU 22-game winning streak, which dated back to 1967. Michigan dominated the ground game, as it rushed for 266 yards and yielded 22 yards, handing Ohio State the defeat.

OSU had to share the conference title after the loss. No Rose Bowl. No national title aspirations. Only next year.

"Be always on the watch, and pray that you may be able to escape all that is about to happen, and that you may be able to stand before the Son of Man."

—LUKE 21:36

4th and 1: You are ten-feet tall and bulletproof. Your dream job is a reality. You possess the best car around and a perfect house. You are convinced you go to church enough to please God. In fact, you feel as if you do the Lord a favor when you show up in His house. Have you ever felt that way? While coasting through your perfect life, have you ever entered a day unprepared to meet the Lord? It's easy to see how this can happen. Life can be busy and demand our time. But you still should maintain and execute a successful daily game plan in order to live a victorious Christian life. The devil has a strategy, and he wants to catch you off guard.

Goal Line Stand: You just entered into a situation you know you can handle. After all, you are No. 1 in your mind. No one can defeat you. No one can stop you in your quest to reach your goal. Wrong! Out of nowhere you get sacked for a loss with no timeouts. The clock winds down, and you must huddle with the Lord—at once. Here are some tips you can take to avoid a sticky predicament. But first, the ego must be tossed out the door so you can take a few bites of an unpleasant dish called humble pie.

1. Pray every day. Find time to be alone with God and give Him your attention. Prayer must be personal with the Lord, and you need to block out all distractions for a few minutes. It can be done if you want, and if it's important enough, you will make the necessary accommodations. Prayer puts you in a healthier state of mind, and you will be able to see the shifts in the enemy's defenses.

2. Read the Bible each day. There you will find the essentials to fend off bad thoughts or temptations. The Scriptures are a road map for success—they are the believer's play-

book and must be followed in order to win the game of life. Set aside the same time every day to read the Word of God. Consider the purchase of a devotional, which can assist you in a goal to read through the entire Bible at a steady pace.

3. <u>Show gratitude.</u> When you are thankful for what you own, it will help you establish a positive attitude. People around you love encouragement, and there is no better way to demonstrate that characteristic than with a thankful heart. God has blessed you with a home, a family, a job, health, a church, a nation, etc. Appreciate all the Lord has done for you each day.

4. <u>Forgive others.</u> You will be penalized 15 yards if you hold a grudge. If someone does you wrong, it's understandable to be upset. But at the end of the day, you must forgive. You might use the experience to remember and be cautious, but if you give someone a second chance, you will get closer to the end zone and set your life up for a score.

5. <u>Help people.</u> Put yourself last and your neighbor first. When you do this, it will feel like you returned a kickoff for a touchdown, the most exciting play in football.

Go into each day with a game plan. Never underestimate the opponent. Refuse to look ahead to the next contest. Planning is fine, but you first need to incorporate a game-strategy. Then, follow through—execute.

DAY 13

Connect Deep in Prayer

August 30, 2014: Ohio State 34, Navy 17

"Trust in the Lord with all your heart and lean not on your own understanding; in all your ways submit to him, and he will make your paths straight."

—PROVERBS 3:5-6

The first game of the 2014 season did not go as planned for Head Coach Urban Meyer. He anticipated his Buckeyes would put the game out of reach in the first half. Instead, Ohio State struggled on the offensive end. They could not find any rhythm and trailed Navy 14-13 midway through the third quarter.

OSU started a drive on its own 20-yard line. First and 10. An enormous play needed to energize the fans who wore Scarlet and Gray in Baltimore, Maryland.

Quarterback J.T. Barrett dropped back to pass, stepped up in the pocket and delivered a soft touch to Devin Smith, who sprinted to the end zone for an 80-yard touchdown. Just like that, the momentum shifted, and the Bucks went on to win the game 34-17. In the blink of an eye it all came together.

Are you ready? When you are a believer in Christ, you must be on watch for His return. He will come like a thief in the night. You cannot afford to let a distraction keep you from your final destination of Heaven.

"For he has rescued us from the dominion of darkness and brought us into the kingdom of the Son he loves, in whom we have redemption, the forgiveness of sins."

—COLOSSIANS 1:13-14

4th and 1: Maybe you are in a spiritual struggle. Circumstances outside of your control have kept you out of rhythm. This might cause confusion and make you second guess some decisions you have made in life. Several situations can lead to this condition. You expect God to answer a request, and He hasn't yet. Perhaps a loved one suffers, and you don't know why. No matter the cause, you must stay focused and plow through, or the devil will dominate. He wants you to struggle and not value your relationship with Christ. Finally, maybe you struggle with prayer. You don't feel connected. As a child of God, you must conquer doubt and confusion. A solid prayer life can keep you focused on your receiver headed toward the goal line. Step up and connect with the Lord.

Goal Line Stand: Here are some tips to overcome struggles when you talk with God:

1. Limit or eliminate distractions. A conversation with the Lord is difficult to hold while a television is blaring in the next room. Or there might be people nearby who carry on a conversation while you try to pray. This is all too common. Find a quiet place to commune with God. Close a door or take a drive to a quiet park if you want alone time. Distractions will hinder one-on-one time between you and the Lord.

2. Praise comes first. In order to have an effective and powerful prayer time with the Master, you need to give

Him glory first. He is worthy. Then you can enter into the next phase of your personal time with Jesus.

3. <u>Be specific.</u> The Bible tells us we have not because we ask not. Tell the Lord what you desire. Go into details, and be crystal clear.

4. <u>Seek forgiveness.</u> Tell the Lord you are sorry for the sins you've committed. He will grant forgiveness if you ask with a humble heart.

5. <u>Give thanks.</u> The Lord appreciates your gratitude. Thank Him in advance, and believe He will deliver in the clutch.

A child of God will struggle once in a while. It's natural. Stay in prayer and find your rhythm. And when you need a long touchdown, the Lord will connect with you for the score.

DAY 14

Run the Race to Win

November 11, 1995: Ohio State 41, Illinois 3

"However, I consider my life worth nothing to me; my only aim is to finish the race and complete the task the Lord Jesus has given me—the task of testifying to the good news of God's grace."

—ACTS 20:24

A successful ground game was needed to defeat Illinois. Eddie George fit into a perfect OSU game plan.

The eventual 1995 Heisman Trophy winner delivered in a big way. He plowed through the Illini defense and rushed for 313 yards on 35 carries—with 8.9 yards per carry average—to lead the Buckeyes to a 41-3 win at the Horseshoe.

Ohio State head football coach John Cooper said in a press conference after the game he had never seen a better individual performance. "He came to play today and did a great job with every opportunity," Cooper stated. "If Eddie George isn't the finest football player in nation and deserving of the Heisman Trophy, I don't know who is."

Ohio State held a 17-0 advantage at the break. George came out with a bang to start the third period and dashed 64-yards for the score. He ran for 105 yards in that quarter alone.

The Fighting Illini Head Coach Lou Tepper also acknowledged George's tremendous performance in front of

93,000 people, and called the running back spectacular and a nightmare at the same time.

George's performance topped the one by Buckeye legend Keith Byars, who rushed for 274 yards against Illinois on October 14, 1984.

> *"Do you not know that in a race all the runners run, but only one gets the prize? Run in such a way as to get the prize. Everyone who competes in the games goes into strict training. They do it to get a crown that will not last, but we do it to get a crown that will last forever."*

> —1 CORINTHIANS 9:24-25

4th and 1: The Christian race is similar to the great performance of Eddie George. Because of his fantastic season, he took home college football's most prestigious trophy. The award goes to the most outstanding player each year. When you are a Christian, your race can be compared to a marathon. But like George, you need to be in shape spiritually and prepared for the defense.

Goal Line Stand: Your opponent for the next game is the devil. In fact, you face him every day of your life. The game plan must be simple and to the point. There can be no razzle-dazzle plays. He must be dealt with in a firm way. You must be prepared to run straight up the middle and let the Lord be your lead blocker. The race takes determination and focus. Here are some tips to establish a successful game strategy:

1. <u>Run the race to win.</u> This seems obvious, but some people who participate in marathons just want to finish the event. Although this goal is admirable, a Christian must possess the mindset to win the spiritual race.

2. <u>Be disciplined and train well.</u> Make sure you have devotions and attend church services on a regular basis. It will make you stronger and assure a winning season.

3. <u>Never, ever look back.</u> Once the Lord has forgiven you of your sins, put the past behind you. Stare ahead at the prize you will receive. John Wayne once said, "Looking back is a bad habit." When you glance behind you, it will distract you from your ultimate goal, which is ahead of you.

4. <u>Be with people who encourage you.</u> If you hang with friends who try to drag you down, find new ones. Deliver encouragement first, and you will receive it. When you speak positive messages, people notice and they will do the same.

5. <u>Break the chains.</u> For example, if you were an alcoholic before God delivered you, do not visit a bar or even eat in a place that serves liquor. If you were addicted to a harmful substance, remove the temptation and seek help. Ask God to open new doors for you and close the old ones. Staying near to God will keep you strong enough to resist.

6. <u>Keep the finish line in view.</u> When you run your race, try to envision the end goal. This will keep you motivated and encouraged. Anticipate a wonderful prize at the end of the event. This should be enough to keep you focused. Know why you are there. For George, his actions symbolized and announced to the entire world he was the best player in college football. When you are a believer, your prize will be a robe and crown once you cross the finish line into Heaven.

There might be times when the defense might blitz and throw you for a loss. Regroup and design a play in the huddle you are confident will earn substantial results. Pray for rescue from the setbacks and, rest assured, the Lord will carry you over the goal line when you stay focused on the prize.

DAY 15

Never, Ever Give Up

October 28, 1989: Ohio State 41, Minnesota 37

"But as for you, be strong and do not give up, for your work will be rewarded."

—*2 CHRONICLES 15:7*

The easy way out would have been to leave at halftime and head back to Columbus. After all, the Buckeyes trailed 31-0 to host Minnesota with a few minutes left in the first half.

Ohio State gave the ball away four times in the first two quarters. They did not play well and stared a blow-out right in the face. But OSU quarterback Greg Frey orchestrated an 80-yard drive for a score at the end of the half to put his squad on the board 31-8. The odds were against the Bucks' chances to be victorious. The team trailed by 23 points, and the offense was not in sync.

Adjustments were made at the intermission. The Buckeyes put 10 points on the board in the third stanza and tallied 23 points in the final period.

Frey made the difference as he compiled 327 yards in the air in the second half alone to lead the Scarlet and Gray to the Big Ten Conference and come-from-behind win.

"I have fought the good fight, I have finished the race, I have kept the faith."

—*2 TIMOTHY 4:7*

In this game called life, have you felt hopeless at times?

4th and 1: An easy way out for Ohio State would have been to surrender. The players could have just gone through the motions in the second half to get the game over. A 31-0 deficit appeared to be too much of a task to overcome. Why not go home?

Like the Buckeyes, you will encounter times when you feel there's no way to recover from a terrible incident. The devil wants you to quit. Maybe you think God and others cannot forgive you. That is not the case with the Lord. You can make the resurgence. Seek forgiveness, give your game plan to Christ, and let Him make the calls from the press box. You can overcome the odds and walk a victorious faith-filled life.

Goal Line Stand: You are faced with a situation that could change your life. Perhaps you experienced a personal tragedy. Maybe your spouse left you, or your child rejected you as a parent. The doctor presented you with a serious diagnosis. Your faith is put to the test, and Satan has a huge halftime lead. The odds of recovery from this setback are bad. You feel like you want to give up and hide from the world. You are not alone in this battle. Christians go through pain too. But children of God have some tools to help through the dark times:

1. God vowed He will never leave you. Take His commitment to you serious and stake your claim on the Word every day. Shadrach, Meshach and Abednego braved horrible odds when they were tossed into a fiery furnace. What happened? God came through and rescued them. You must possess fierce faith that He will deliver you from your trial. Even when the flames get close and

you can feel the scorching heat, you must believe on the Lord's promises to protect you from harm.

2. Increase your prayer life. The Bible instructs you to pray without ceasing. Be in a prayerful state of mind throughout the day. Spend a few extra moments in conversation with the Lord, but be sure to listen too. Let Him guide you in all you do.

3. Increase your praise. God has blessed you in countless ways. In turn, give Him glory. A simple testimony of thanks to Jesus for an answered prayer will make you stronger.

4. Rebuke the enemy. This is a vital step in your growth. If the devil knows he has you in a weakened state, call on the name of the Lord. Make the enemy flee faster than a safety blitz.

No matter the circumstance, remember God loves you. That is enough motivation to inspire a fourth-quarter comeback.

DAY 16

Fight the Good Fight

January 2, 2015: Ohio State 42, Alabama 35

"Blessed is the one who perseveres under trial because, having stood the test, that person will receive the crown of life that the Lord has promised to those who love him."

—JAMES 1:12

Ohio State needed a score in a bad way. The team trailed high-powered Alabama 21-6 in the Sugar Bowl midway through the second period. Buckeye tailback Ezekiel Elliott made his way to the end zone to narrow the Crimson Tide's lead to 21-13.

Just prior to the half, OSU had the ball on the Alabama 13-yard line on second down. Wide receiver Evan Spencer took a reverse pitch and fired a tight spiral pass to Michael Thomas in the front corner of the end zone. Thomas got a foot inbounds and brought the Buckeyes to within one point before the half. This play was the key point in the game as a motivated Ohio State came out and dominated the second half.

Elliott sealed the win with 3:24 left in the game when he scampered 85 yards for a TD to give OSU a 42-28 lead. Ohio State defeated Alabama 42-35 to claim the Sugar Bowl crown in New Orleans and advance to the first ever College Football National Championship playoff game.

The Bucks demonstrated the confidence to prevail. All they had to do was continue to fight.

> *"Fight the good fight of the faith. Take hold of the eternal life to which you were called when you made your good confession in the presence of many witnesses."*
>
> —1 TIMOTHY 6:12

Have you ever found yourself in a fight between right and wrong?

4th and 1: Christians are humans and encounter struggles every day. The key is to stay strong and not surrender. Find a way to punch the ball into the end zone and gain momentum for the next battle. The war against sin is a constant struggle. Take one fight at a time and defeat the enemy, keeping him on the run.

Goal Line Stand: Have you faced a battle and needed momentum to carry you through the next day? When this happens again, remember these three suggestions:

1. Acknowledge your sin. Be honest with yourself and realize your own vulnerabilities. The enemy knows what makes you weak, and chances are you do too. Pride, lust, selfishness, anger, dishonesty, or cheating might be your kryptonite. In order to allow God to help you fight the good fight, you must know the strength of your sin.

2. Allow God to fight your battles. Your mistakes and weaknesses will often attempt to rise up and destroy you. As a child of God, you must claim victory through Christ and ask Him to forgive your transgressions. Pray to God for the willpower to shut off the computer or to

ignore a phone call. Determination to do what is right makes you stronger in the Lord.

3. Put your full trust in the Lord. Remember, Jesus won the battle over sin when he was crucified, buried, and arose from the grave. You must remind yourself what the Lord did for you and what he will do through you. He finished His work on the cross. Trust what He says, and remember the game has already been won. You are along for this ride called life. Make sure everyone you meet gets a chance to play on the same team.

We endure obstacles each day from the forces of evil. Some battles might be against a computer screen while other battles might be emotional. Thoughts of loneliness or lack of self-worth are also real struggles people withstand. Satan may use sickness or financial hardship to try to defeat you. No matter the enemy, find comfort in the fact Jesus won the greatest championship of all time. And one day you will raise the trophy at the end of your game.

DAY 17

Make an Impact as a Christian

January 2, 2015: Ohio State 42, Alabama 35

"You are the light of the world. A town built on a hill cannot be hidden."

—MATTHEW 5:14

You do not need a lot of attention to make your presence known. You can do it without a lot of noise. Take for instance, Evan Spencer, Ohio State wide receiver. He performed his job well and reaped praise and reward.

The No. 4 ranked Buckeyes led No. 1 ranked Alabama by six points in the fourth quarter in the Sugar Bowl. A trip to the College Football Playoff National Championship was on the line, and the OSU offense sputtered.

Once again, they were deep in their own territory with the ball. Alabama hoped to receive the ball from a punt. A big play was essential for the Bucks to climb out of the hole and give themselves more room to breathe.

OSU had the ball on its own 15-yard line on first down. QB Cardale Jones gave the ball to tailback Ezekiel Elliott, who ran off left tackle. Spencer came in from the wide receiver position and took out two Bama defenders, springing Elliott loose for an 85-yard sprint to score and decide the outcome.

Ohio State went on to win the game against Alabama in New Orleans, 42-35.

Had Spencer not done his job on that particular play, Elliott would have been stopped. He rose to the occasion as he did all game long. Spencer delivered a perfectly-timed and effective block, and he also came through with other fantastic plays that day.

Earlier in the game, he threw a TD pass to Michael Thomas for a score that changed the momentum of the contest. He also made a spectacular one-handed grab from a Jones throw but was out of bounds. He later sealed the deal for the Buckeyes when he out-jumped Alabama's ArDarius Stewart and grabbed the on-side kick to finalize the victory. The overall impact he made throughout the game resulted in a Buckeye defeat of Alabama.

What influence do you have that can make a difference in others?

> *"For the spirit God gave us does not make us timid, but gives us power, love, and self-discipline."*

> —2 TIMOTHY 1:7

4th and 1: Everyone wants to be productive. Some desire the limelight for their actions more than others. Many take pride in a job well done. Recognition is nice but not necessary. Spencer knew his role and delivered when called upon. He performed the assigned responsibilities without fanfare, but he stood out to those who watched the game. Are you happy to just be a good influence on others, or do you prefer the entire world to know?

Goal Line Stand: To demonstrate a positive impact on those around you, first make sure you are prepared to play. Here are some tips of advice to make sure you are ready on game-day:

1. Help people. Put aside your own wants and desires, and focus on those who cry out for assistance. When you take the time to help a friend through a tough time, you can look yourself in the mirror and know you had the strength to put others first.

2. Treat others how you wish to be treated. The Golden Rule is not just an old saying, it always applies. When you master the art of kindness to those who are not kind to you, then you might be ready to enter the game.

3. Read the Bible each day. In the Word of God, you will find what you need to feed your soul and mind. Try to reserve at least 10 or 20 minutes a day to read and enjoy God speaking to you through the Bible. Set a goal to read it through in a year.

4. Give thanks. Be grateful for what you possess—and even what you don't. Sometimes blessings come from what you lack.

5. Forgive. This is essential in your successful walk with the Lord. You may find mercy difficult to give, but at the end of the day, you must forgive others to keep sweet peace in your heart.

6. Pray. Frequent communication with the Lord is a must. You find time to talk to your spouse, children, parents, and friends. Talk to the Master, and don't forget to listen to Him too.

7. <u>Share the wonderful news.</u> The Lord expects His children to tell others about Him. Invite people to worship with you. Expose them to the gospel in the best way possible.

If you follow these suggestions, you will be ready and equipped to step onto the field and make the plays that win ballgames. You might not receive the MVP, but you will earn a robe and crown in Heaven.

DAY 18

Protect Your House

January 2, 2015: Ohio State 42, Alabama 35

"May the Lord answer you when you are in distress; may the name of the God of Jacob protect you."

—PSALM 20:1

The No. 4 ranked Ohio State Buckeyes came out strong in the second half of the Sugar Bowl against No. 1 ranked Alabama. A 47-yard touchdown strike by quarterback Cardale Jones put OSU in front 27-21.

Late in the third quarter, the mighty Crimson Tide was faced with a third down and seven yards to go from its own 36-yard line. When the ball was snapped for an obvious pass, Ohio State defensive end Steve Miller dropped back in coverage. Alabama QB Blake Simms attempted a pass and was picked off by Miller, who then darted into the end zone to give the Bucks a 34-21 lead.

The defensive play stymied the high-powered Bama offense. On the other hand, OSU's offense kicked into high gear. Jones was described as a battering ram with a cannon attached to his shoulder. He and ball carrier Ezekiel Elliott carried the load for OSU. Jones made big plays while Elliott rushed for 230 yards and two TDs. Ohio State secured the Sugar Bowl with a 42-35 upset win, and the victory put them into the inaugural College Football Playoff National Championship game.

The defensive play Miller made set the tone. He protected his turf and did not allow the enemy to penetrate.

"The righteous person may have many troubles, but the Lord delivers him from them all."

—PSALM 34:19

4th and 1: Every person longs for safety and security. Most parents will do whatever it takes to make sure their children and property are safe. Perhaps you don't have children but your parents are still alive, and you want that same security for them when they grow older. The natural instinct is to guard and protect your family. When a mama bear suspects her cubs are in danger, look out. She will destroy any threat to her little ones. The Lord feels the same way about you. He hates when the devil comes at us and puts us in a dangerous circumstance. He will do what it takes to assure our safety. Do you feel that way too? What will you do to protect your loved ones from Satan?

Goal Line Stand: Prayer is the best action you can take to ensure safety for your loved ones from the forces of evil. A special request you can make of the Lord is to form a hedge of protection around your loved ones. This kind of prayer consists of three parts:

1. <u>Petition the Lord to rebuke and bind the power of the devil from each member of your family.</u> Request Him to release any strongholds Satan may take in your life and in the lives of your loved ones. Be specific and turn them over to the Master.

2. <u>Pray these requests in the name of Jesus Christ.</u> The Bible tells us in a matter-of-fact way—whatever we ask in His name, He will do. The hardest part might be to wait. He will answer in His time. Ohio State fans might have wanted Miller to make an impactful play sooner, but it came at just the right time. The Lord will answer for you in the same way.

3. <u>Stake a claim and grip tight to the commitments made in scripture.</u> This can be used in several situations such as to safeguard you from sin or from personal emotions, like depression or anxiety. Take comfort—the Lord will never leave nor forsake you or your family. This is important to remember while you pray for the safety of your household.

One of the most important actions a parent or friend can take behind the scenes is to ask for protection for your family. Be confident the Master will go to great lengths to demonstrate His power and commitment to you. Be patient and show love, but be vigilant—drop in the zone and be ready to intercept any pass from the devil.

DAY 19

Be an Encouragement to Others

November 22, 2014: Ohio State 42, Indiana 27

"Love the Lord, all his faithful people! The Lord preserves those who are true to him, but the proud he pays back in full."

—PSALM 31:23

The faithful fans at the Horseshoe in Columbus appeared restless. What most expected to be a blowout developed into a close-knit game. In fact, the host Buckeyes fell behind Indiana. How could this be? Indiana, of all teams, was out in front 20-14 late in the third quarter.

Ohio State's special teams emerged to be important when punter Cameron Johnston pinned Indiana inside its own five-yard line. Now it was the defense's turn to dominate. The Hoosiers were held to a three-and-out and forced to punt from deep within their own end zone.

Buckeye receiver Jalin Marshall took the punt on the OSU 54-yard line and dashed right down the middle of the field for the dramatic go-ahead score with 2:12 left in third period. He was far from done and caught three more TD passes from quarterback J.T. Barrett in the final quarter, and the Bucks put Indiana away 42-27. His big-time play at the right moment encouraged the OSU faithful who wore Scarlet and Gray.

"But I will not take my love from him, nor will I ever betray my faithfulness."

—PSALM 89:33

Do you do enough to encourage others around you?

4th and 1: Ask yourself these questions. Do you encourage others? Do you deliver when called upon by your church or family? Do you do enough to lead your team ahead of the enemy? These are difficult and impactful questions all Christians must ask of themselves. No one likes to lose, and you must portray a never-die attitude. When the heat is on from the forces of evil and those closest to you grow agitated, what action do you take?

Goal Line Stand: Have your loved ones acted a bit anxious in recent days? Perhaps a national tragedy or a natural disaster put them on edge. Take your spot to receive the punt and go all the way for the score. Here are some tips to encourage those near you:

1. <u>For no reason, give a small gift to a person</u> just to show appreciation and love.

2. <u>Send a card of encouragement to a friend</u> who might be in the middle of a difficult time. A quick note to let them know they are in your prayers might be just what is needed.

3. <u>Listen to a friend's concerns,</u> and do not talk about yourself.

4. <u>Send a devotional or a scripture through email or a text.</u> Keep them short and simple. A note of encouragement will do.

5. <u>Give genuine compliments to a friend.</u> You don't have to go overboard; a modest acknowledgment will suffice.

6. <u>Take a friend who feels dejected out for a cup of coffee.</u> The time you take will be more valuable to your friend than the coffee.

7. <u>Offer a "thank you" and "have a nice day" to those you meet.</u> You may not know how your simple, kind words might impact the other person's day.

8. <u>Pay for a stranger's meal</u> in a restaurant without them knowing.

9. <u>Stop and visit a widow or widower</u> to let them know you care. This can brighten their week.

10. <u>Rake the leaves for your neighbors, or some other task that demands attention.</u> Reach out and tell them you want to help. Your witness will be strengthened, and people will see Christ in your actions.

The overall objective is to allow people to witness Christ in you. When you donate your time, which is your most valuable commodity, it will not go unnoticed. This may seem small to you but not to the person who benefits from it. Give your time because it will mean more than a go-ahead punt return for a touchdown.

DAY 20

Sacrifice Everything to the Lord

November 29, 2014: Ohio State 42, Michigan 28

"But God demonstrates his own love for us in this: While we were still sinners, Christ died for us."

—ROMANS 5:8

Faithful fans at the Horseshoe in Columbus were thrilled. The Buckeyes scored on their first possession against their rival Michigan. However, the OSU offense stalled while the Wolverines picked up and took a 14-7 lead toward the end of the second period.

Ohio State had the ball on the Michigan 25-yard line with 17 seconds left in the half. Quarterback J.T. Barrett dropped to pass. He scanned the field and could not find an open receiver. He scampered into the end zone for a score to tie the game right before the break.

Barrett proved to be a legitimate contender for the Heisman Trophy. During the game, he completed 13 of 21 passes for 176 yards with a touchdown. On the ground, he gained 89 yards and scored two times on 15 carries. He was the lifeblood of the offense.

The same crowd that cheered on the Bucks was silenced toward the end of the game. The 108,000 people who packed out Ohio Stadium witnessed Barrett suffer a broken ankle. Ohio State won the game, but victory came at an expense.

Have you ever been puzzled by developments that arose that seemed totally opposite to what you thought would happen? Remember—God has a plan for everyone.

"And do not forget to do good and to share with others, for with such sacrifices God is pleased."

—HEBREWS 13:16

4th and 1: Maybe life is magnificent for you and your family. A large raise came your way, and the truck you have had your eye on went on sale. Your friends threw a surprise birthday party for you, and you have planned a lavish vacation. All is right in the world. Then BOOM! You are sideswiped with horrible news. Your company announces plans to restructure and lay off workers. The new truck you bought the other day has mechanical problems. A close friend was diagnosed with a terminal illness. Now what? In one small moment of time, life can change for the worse. Just like those in attendance who watched their field general go down, you too are in shock. What will happen now? What will you do?

Goal Line Stand: You find it's easy to praise the Lord when life goes your way. Fans take great joy when their team wins. But when circumstances change, the squad depends on the crowd's support more than ever. The same is true when life causes you to fumble in front of the end zone. In that instance, you need God more than ever. You must learn to honor Him in the good times and the bad. Here are some sacrifices you can make each day to prepare for the storms of life:

1. Sacrifice your time. Increase the amount of time you spend in devotions, just a few minutes each day will make a big difference. Volunteer to help a friend or work a shift for a non-profit organization you endorse. The most valuable asset we have is our time. God will honor us when we make a point to give more of ourselves to Him.

2. Sacrifice your desires. The luxuries of the world cannot compare to the rewards in Heaven. This does not mean to sell your possessions, but rather take inventory and notice on what you have placed importance over the Lord. Perhaps you would rather go fishing or golf than attend your church's revival. Which is more important? The Holy Spirit may convict you to put these hobbies on hold for a bit to spend more time with Him. Show the Lord you desire Him more than extracurricular activities.

3. Sacrifice your money. Your resources are from the Lord, everything you have comes from Him. The Bible instructs us to give 10-percent of our income. Why stop there? Make a point to give more. On top of the 10-percent, perhaps consider giving to a charity or pay for a person's groceries or an occasional meal. Think outside of the box. God will reward your generosity.

We can give back to the Lord in various ways. When life gets to be too much and you suffer an inconvenient, emotional, or physical injury—look to the Master. He gave His Son for you. Be willing to give of yourself to others.

DAY 21

Be the Inspiration

January 12, 2015: Ohio State 42, Oregon 20, College Football Playoff National Championship.

"Jesus looked at them and said, 'With man this is impossible, but not with God; all things are possible with God.'"

—MARK 10:27

The No. 4 Ohio State Buckeyes entered the inaugural College Football Playoff National Championship Game as a long shot to win. The team had just knocked off No. 1 Alabama and now faced No. 2 Oregon in Arlington, Texas. Experts predicted a difficult challenge for OSU to beat the number one and number two teams back-to-back with a third-string player under center.

The Ducks made the first move and scored to take a 7-0 lead. The Buckeye offense could not seem to establish a rhythm and was in desperate search for a spark. Midway through the first quarter, Ezekiel Elliott took the handoff from Cardale Jones and broke a few tackles on his 33-yard jaunt to score and tie the game 7-7. The tailback rushed for 248 yards and tallied four touchdowns to lead Ohio State to a 42-20 win over the Ducks for the crown.

The performance was Elliott's third straight effort to rush for more than 200 yards. He gave credit to the offensive line and described the win as a "surreal moment." OSU waited more than a decade to return the title to Columbus. The last National Championship was in 2002, when they defeated Miami.

> *"But those who hope in the Lord will renew their strength. They will soar on wings like eagles; they will run and not grow weary, they will walk and not be faint."*
>
> —ISAIAH 40:31

Elliott reached deep within his soul and inspired the team. He came through at a time when they needed him to perform.

4th and 1: Most people want to do good. Parents above all should strive to inspire their children. Often, young adults put athletes on a pedestal. Others admire people in the entertainment industry as role models. You, too, can be an inspiration to others, although you might not know what actions to take. Here are a few suggestions on how to have a positive impact on others.

Goal Line Stand: To be an inspiration, adopt a humble attitude and spirit. Ask the Lord what you can do. Be ready to accept His answer, even though you may not like what He tells you to do.

1. Share your talents. Every person has a gift. Find your gifts—the things He has placed in you to help others—and use them to glorify the Lord. He will reveal your talents. Maybe you make greeting cards or you garden. Make and send a card to a person who is sick, or take your home-grown flowers to a neighbor. This may not seem much to you, but it may make a huge difference to the recipient.

2. <u>Participate in charity events.</u> Offer your time and energy to help those who are less fortunate. Ask others to join you and take the lead to volunteer. Help others and be an inspiration to those around you.

3. <u>Give your tithes and offerings.</u> Most people do this in private, but it will open areas you never thought possible. Before you put your gift in the offering plate or the mail, hold it, pray, and ask the Lord to bless you with opportunities. He will.

4. <u>Be a leader in your home and community.</u> Don't rule with an iron fist, lead your family in prayer and devotions and take them to church. Your children may rebel and resist, but take them anyway. You are the parent. You are to teach and discipline them when needed. You cannot be a best friend. One day they will reflect on what you did with appreciation.

5. <u>Pray.</u> Ask the Lord to develop and prepare you for an opportunity to inspire your family and others.

Some of these may not happen overnight. The Buckeye faithful waited more than a decade for the championship to return to Columbus. Elliott's inspiration for the team played a key role in the win. Take the lead and be patient. These two traits make a successful combination.

DAY 22

Let Your Light Shine

November 8, 2014: Ohio State 49, Michigan State 28

"Neither do people light a lamp and put it under a bowl. Instead they put it on its stand, and it gives light to everyone in the house."

—MATTHEW 5:15

Ohio State wide receiver Michael Thomas let his light shine in East Lansing, Michigan.

At the start of the Big Ten Conference matchup, turnovers plagued OSU. But somehow the Buckeyes trailed 21-14 at the half. In the third period, the team again gave away the ball, this time deep in its own territory. Michigan State could not take advantage and missed a field goal.

Ohio State took over on its own 21. Quarterback J.T. Barrett made a quick connection with Thomas on a slant route and would not be stopped. He went 79 yards for the score to tie the game and give OSU much needed momentum.

The Bucks won the game 49-28, thanks in part to the spark Thomas gave to the offense. He did not hide under a bushel. He let the talent God gave him shine for the college football world to see.

Do you shine for the Lord? Do you tell people about the goodness of God?

"'You are my witnesses,' declares the Lord, 'and my servant whom I have chosen, so that you may know and believe me and understand that I am he. Before me no god was formed, nor will there be one after me.'"

—ISAIAH 43:10

4th and 1: Life can be hectic when you attend meetings and work at school functions. The hustle and bustle of a day can leave you exhausted. But in times of chaos, do you find opportunities to be a witness for the Lord? Do you make time to be the example you should be to others who do not serve God? Have you fumbled the pigskin a few times like the Buckeyes did in East Lansing? You are not alone. But did you take the slant pass and go the distance when you had the chance? You might be the only Christian a lost person encounters. Will you make the play?

Goal Line Stand: Step up, make the big play, and profess your love for the Lord. Here are a few characteristics a bold representative for Christ can display:

1. Possess a willingness to serve and obey the Lord. Do what Jesus instructs you to do, and let Him lead you to some wonderful opportunities to share the saving grace to others. Serve Christ and let your light shine—what a glorious way to witness.

2. Let your life be blameless. Don't go any place that might embarrass you or your family. Whether you are home or away on a trip, abstain from the very appearance of evil. This helps to avoid traps Satan has set to destroy you.

3. <u>Demonstrate a tender love for others.</u> Show compassion and a concern for your neighbor, and the doors will open to tell them about the Lord's saving grace.

4. <u>Desire to please God, not others.</u> Don't brag on yourself, but rather share what God has done for you. We do not deserve His blessings, and our humble acknowledgement of them goes a lot further than pretension.

5. <u>Show a determination to share the Gospel.</u> Take every available occasion to tell people about the Lord Jesus. You can talk about other topics, such as music or sports, and not delve into your beliefs. But look for ways to insert your Savior into the conversation.

Let your light shine so the Gospel of Christ reflects in you. This will give you the momentum to win the game in a blowout against the enemy.

Day 23

Don't Let the Devil Steal Your Victory

January 1, 1971: Stanford 27, Ohio State 17

"The thief comes only to steal and kill and destroy; I have come that they may have life, and have it to the full."

—JOHN 10:10

Stanford was a 10-point underdog to the Ohio State Buckeyes in the 1971 Rose Bowl.

Quarterback Jim Plunkett proved why he won the Heisman Trophy when he dismantled the OSU defense on the way to the win, Stanford's first Rose Bowl victory in more than 30 years. Not only did OSU lose the prestigious contest, their unbeaten season was spoiled, and their chance to win a national title disappeared.

Plunkett was named the game MVP after he connected on 20 of 30 pass attempts for 265 yards. The Bucks entered the game as the favorite and left defeated.

Has the devil ever tried to steal your victory?

"Jesus turned and said to Peter, 'Get behind me, Satan! You are a stumbling block to me; you do not have in mind the concerns of God, but merely human concerns.'"

—MATTHEW 16:23

4th and 1: The devil uses several tools to lure you away from God. He works to blindside you with his attacks. He wants you to be cocky and take the win for granted. Then out of nowhere he hands you defeat. He is sneaky about his tactics to steal your victory and loves when you lose. He enjoys words which start with the letter D for some reason. Have you ever been *D*istracted, *D*isappointed, *D*iscouraged, *D*epressed, *D*oubtful, or *D*esperate? This is how the devil intends for you to be all the time. When you take on these characteristics, you cannot be an effective witness for the Lord. He tries to steal your joy when you are vulnerable to an attack.

Goal Line Stand: Satan plans to destroy you and everything you represent. He is happy to take your family, too, if he can. Don't let that happen. Execute the game plan below, and take the victory back where it belongs:

1. Realize you are in a battle. Take the devil seriously, and be aware you are no match for him alone. Once you know this, you can seek help from your coach—the Lord.

2. The Bible *must* be your playbook. You cannot stray away from what it teaches. The Word of God must be followed to the T if you are to be victorious in your Christian walk.

3. Desire to obtain wisdom. You may know a great deal about the Bible, but you may struggle to apply its instruction to your day-to-day life. Read Proverbs and you will often find the perfect encouragement.

4. Resist temptation. First, you must know your weakness because the devil already does. Do not be in denial about what distracts you. Get rid of the source, and turn it over to the Lord for destruction. You might think you can control the problem, but you are no competition for Satan without God's help.

5. Be humble. Stay conscious that you can be defeated. Members of a good team know their ability to win but

also have a genuine fear of defeat, which becomes a motivator. Humility shows you are teachable. When a person loses that edge, the door opens for defeat.

6. Always be on guard. The devil knows when you grow weary in your journey. He likes to attack when you become discouraged or depressed. Know the warning signs and be aware of the threat of an assault from the devil. He stands ready to fire a spiritual missile at your heart. He does not play fair, and you must always be ready for him to strike at any moment.

7. Portray a prayerful spirit. When you feel the attack is imminent, increase your communication with God. Rebuke the forces of evil in Jesus' name.

8. Know your limits. You alone are no match for the devil. He knows you are easy to handle once you are away from the Lord. A prowling lion will hunt the young and the weak— those who will not put up much of a fight. Realize you cannot do this alone. Let the Lord fend off the devil.

9. Glorify your Master. Worship God on a regular basis to increase your power over the devil. He hates when we praise the Lord and often flees from the very mention of Jesus' name. When you give glory to God, you become stronger and able to recognize the caution signals of an attack.

10. Be thankful. The Lord Jesus has defeated death, Hell, and the grave, and this reminder is enough to keep you focused on the game plan and win. Do not give the devil any chance to triumph. Do not let him steal your victory.

DAY 24

Show Honor to the Lord

September 30, 1972: Ohio State 29, North Carolina 14

"The Sovereign Lord is my strength; he makes my feet like the feet of a deer, he enable me to tread on the heights."

—HABAKKUK 3:19

Archie Griffin burst onto the scene at Ohio State. The freshman running back from Columbus, Ohio, made his mark in Buckeye history when he ran for 239 yards against unbeaten North Carolina in front of more than 86,000 people.

OSU's offense sputtered before Griffin entered the game. Fans did not know what to expect, but he gave them a taste of what was to come. By halftime, he had racked up 111 yards on 16 carries. He boosted the Buckeyes to a 9-7 lead.

He didn't stop there and poured it on the Tar Heel defense for 128 more yards. In the third quarter, he dazzled everyone with a nine-yard scamper which featured a tight-rope skip along the left side out-of-bounds line into the end zone. Fans loved him right away when he passed the previous record of yards rushed in a game by Ollie Cline, who posted 229 yards in 1945 against Pitt.

After the 29-14 win over North Carolina, Griffin, a 5-10, 185-pound tailback, showed signs of a veteran as he gave credit to the offensive line. His work ethic on the field combined with humility made him one of the iconic players in OSU history.

He is the lone player in college football to win the Heisman Trophy twice. A quiet leader who epitomized effort and hustle, he was a winner on the field and off.

"Lord, be gracious to us; we long for you. Be our strength every morning, our salvation in times of distress."

—ISAIAH 33:2

4th and 1: Do you make your presence known when you are at church or at work? Do you give honor and glory to the Lord or to yourself? Christians are obligated to honor the Lord, not just in a church service where it is easy to praise God. He gave His life for you. Examine yourself and determine if you always show genuine respect for the Lord.

Goal Line Stand: You need to make sure you praise the Lord, and He needs to be at the center of your life. There may be moments when it seems harder to worship than others. However, these three tips might encourage you to honor the Lord more often:

1. Honor the Lord in your home. Make sure your house is a place where Jesus would feel comfortable if he popped in for a visit. What you keep hidden in your heart will show in your house. The same must be for friends and family. You want your residence to be a place where you magnify the Master. A large Bible on the coffee table is fine, but it takes more than that to display how much you love the Savior. Do not give people any reason to doubt. Show the light of Jesus in your home, and this will give you confidence to profess Him in public.

2. <u>Honor the Lord in your spirit.</u> Take part in devotions and conversations with Him each day. Make time to be alone with Jesus Christ, and you will draw closer in your relationship. You demonstrate solid character when you do what's right and honest in private, not only in public. Never give in to Satan's temptations, even when no one is around to watch. Meditate on God in those times, and honor Him and you will have perfect peace.

3. <u>Honor the Lord in every opportunity.</u> Tell others about the goodness of God's grace when you see the chance. You can carry on a secular conversation about the weather or the Ohio State Buckeyes, but people should know you are a believer when the conversation is finished. Find a way to sprinkle your faith into the mix. What a great way to score.

Strive to be a positive and immediate influence for others. But first, honor the Lord in all you do. This way, people will remember your name too.

DAY 25

It's Not About You

January 8, 2007: Florida 41, Ohio State 14, National Championship

"Do nothing out of selfish ambition or vain conceit. Rather, in humility value others above yourselves, not looking to your own interests but each of you to the interests of the others."

—PHILIPPIANS 2:3-4

The No. 1 ranked Ohio State Buckeyes came out of the gates on a mission. Their dynamic kick returner Ted Ginn Jr. sent a statement to the No. 2 Florida Gators and opened the game with a 93-yard kickoff return. Within a few seconds, OSU took a 7-0 lead.

He had done this several times. The receiver previously took two kickoffs for touchdowns and six punts in his career. No Florida defender touched the former high school track star. All the Gators saw was a scarlet and gray streak. He led the team during the season with 59 catches for 781 yards and nine TDs, and was a vital part of the offensive plan.

But after he raced into the end zone, he became injured as he celebrated and had to leave the game. He would not play anymore that night. When the second half started, he limped on the sideline on crutches with a black boot on the injured left foot. The touchdown play was important, but the celebration came at a high cost. Florida went on to crush the Bucks 41-14 to win the National Championship.

The game commenced with extreme promise for OSU and ended with dejection. An ill-advised celebration hindered the team's chances to win the game. A celebration is fine once the task has been completed, but in this case, it was premature.

Do you claim victory and draw attention to yourself before the job gets done?

> *"Those who live according to the flesh have their minds set on what the flesh desires; but those who live in accordance with the Spirit have their minds set on what the Spirit desires."*

> —ROMANS 8:5

4th and 1: Celebrations are good if they don't go over the top and draw unnecessary attention to you. There are appropriate times to give yourself a high-five for a job well done. However, when life becomes all about you, problems arise. Do you like attention? Do you want to be the life of the party and be recognized?

Goal Line Stand: Modesty and humility are fantastic qualities to demonstrate. When the time comes to celebrate an earned achievement, acknowledge others who helped along the way. Don't make it about you. Here are a few tips on how to stay humble:

1. <u>Serve others.</u> When you do this, you fulfill God's purpose in your life. Put the focus on the kingdom of God rather than yourself.

2. <u>Demonstrate a grateful heart.</u> The more you develop an attitude of thanks for the gift of salvation, the more you will have revealed about His love.

3. <u>Die to self.</u> We may be proud of ourselves when we achieve what we deem a great accomplishment. However, we must strive to die to ourselves each day and live through our Lord with humility.

4. <u>Admit when you are wrong.</u> There are times in life when you are not right. Acknowledge this with an open mind. Take criticism with grace, and ask the Lord to show you a better way to react than with anger and hostility.

5. <u>Forgive quickly.</u> When someone hurts you, show mercy and love. I would even challenge you to pray for them.

6. <u>Give with sincerity.</u> One of the cornerstones of Christianity is to help others who are without. When you give an item of value to a person who is less fortunate, God notices, and He will bless you for your sacrifice. Do this in private and without fanfare.

If Ted Ginn Jr. had just tossed the ball to the official and high-fived his teammates, he might not have been injured in an end zone celebration. Who knows what the outcome might have been? While he might not take the full blame for the loss, his actions hurt the Buckeyes—the team needed him to play. Put pride and celebrations aside and do your job as a Christian with peace and strength. Others will take note.

DAY 26

<u>Take Back Your Joy</u>

January 3, 2003: Ohio State 31, Miami 24
2OT National Championship

"Restore to me the joy of your salvation and grant me a willing spirit to sustain me."

—PSALM 51:12

The No. 2 ranked Ohio State Buckeyes were considerable underdogs to mighty No. 1 ranked Miami. During the season, the Hurricanes blew away their opponents and outscored them 503-217. But Ohio State took a 14-7 lead into the half thanks to touchdown runs from field general Craig Krenzel and tailback Maurice Clarett.

The third quarter started with a solid OSU march through the field to the Canes' six-yard line. The signal caller spotted the tight end Ben Hartsock in the end zone. But Miami's Sean Taylor picked off the pass and had a clear shot for the 100-yard return. For a split second, a score seemed inevitable.

But out of nowhere, Clarett came to the rescue. He tackled Taylor and somehow snatched the ball away to reclaim possession for the Bucks on the 22-yard line. No doubt, he made the play of the game. He stopped a potential score by the opponent and gave his team the opportunity to advance.

OSU went on to win 31-24 in double overtime and claim the national title in Tempe, Arizona. Their first national championship since 1970 came despite the fact they were outgained 369 yards to 267. Many call it the best college championship game ever played.

> *"I have told you this so that my joy may be in you and that your joy may be complete."*
>
> —JOHN 15:11

Has the devil intercepted your joy? What are you going to do to fight back?

4th and 1: Perhaps you used to be happy and never questioned God. But along the way, circumstances changed. Maybe someone hurt you. The devil uses several strategies to sidetrack us. He loves to pick off our happiness and take it to the house for a score. Once he does, he will spike the pigskin right in our face.

Goal Line Stand: If your days are sad, you must act fast, just like Clarett did. If he had not chased Taylor down, the entire momentum of the game might have shifted. Here are some steps you can take to wrestle the ball away from Satan:

1. Don't worry about the future. The Lord is clear when He tells us in His Word not to fret about what lies ahead. If you doubt God's power to take care of you, you will lose your joy.

2. Do not agonize over events of the past. Leave yesterday behind and move forward. You cannot undo what has been done. If you make a mistake, learn to grow from it and determine never to repeat it again.

3. <u>Do not procrastinate.</u> If Clarett put off the tackle, the Buckeyes may not have won. Don't delay to help those in need. If the Lord tells you to visit a friend who is ill, obey Him. The moment may not present itself again.

4. <u>Do not compare yourself to others.</u> You are God's special design, and He gave you talents and gifts to use for His glory.

5. <u>Do not focus on the negatives and your problems.</u> Leave your troubles behind you and ask the Lord to take care of them. This does not mean to ignore a bill when money is short, but depend on God to provide an opportunity to praise Him.

If you follow these suggestions, you will develop a more positive attitude and rejoice in His blessings. When the devil tries to intercept your joy, take it away from him and run for the goal. Take comfort and know you are on God's victorious team.

DAY 27

Be a Dependable Member of the Team

October 19, 2002: Ohio State 19, Wisconsin 14

"Whoever can be trusted with very little can also be trusted with much, and whoever is dishonest with very little will also be dishonest with much."

—LUKE 16:10

The No. 4 ranked Buckeyes went into Madison, Wisconsin, while skeptics murmured about the strength of their schedule. The team was 8-0 on the season and stared a berth at the National Title game right in the eye.

Tough contests lay ahead against Michigan and Penn State. OSU stood 3-0 in the Big Ten Conference, but they knew the Badgers planned to stage a fight at Camp Randall Stadium. Wisconsin had an upset in mind. Their record was 5-3 overall and 0-3 in the conference, but they somehow took a 14-13 lead against Ohio State in the fourth quarter.

About 10 minutes were left to play in the game when quarterback Craig Krenzel connected with tight end Ben Hartsock for the go-ahead touchdown. The Bucks prevailed 19-14 in a hard-fought contest.

After the game, Hartsock said he used his entire body to haul in the catch. "It was like there was a baby in there," he said. Once again, he proved to be in the right place at the right time. Always dependable as a Buckeye, the 6'4", 265-pound tight end from Chillicothe, Ohio, had a solid career with the Scarlet and Gray. Over four years, he caught 57 passes for 515 yards for a 9.0 average. He also scored five crucial TDs. But his ability to block and positive attitude to play a role stood out to several coaches and fans, and he was named to the OSU All-Decade Team.

Complete team players are often a key to a team's success. When a player is comfortable and happy to work behind the scenes, that says a lot about his character.

> *"Whatever happens, conduct yourselves in a manner worthy of the gospel of Christ. Then, whether I come and see you or only hear about you in my absence, I will know that you stand firm in the one Spirit, striving together as one for the faith of the gospel."*
>
> —PHILIPPIANS 1:27

Does this verse describe you?

4th and 1: Perhaps a friend asked you to take part in an activity at church which will not get much attention. Or maybe you visit sick people, and nobody knows but them. Whatever the case, people have learned to depend on you to come through in the clutch. You never receive applause or recognition, and you are good with that. A successful athlete will once in a while take a back seat to a superstar. In due time, however, the person who lurks in the shadow will one day be brought to the light.

Goal Line Stand: Be someone others can depend on to come through in tough times at work, home, or church. God is dependable, you can trust Him to be there for you. If you're new to being a player for God, here are some tips on trusting Him:

1. Give up. Surrender your wants and needs to the Master. Once you put Him first, He will direct you in a path to help others and be a dependable Christian. This is not easy and requires you to sacrifice any ego you may possess.

2. Follow and walk with Christ. On your journey with Him, you will learn important lessons. Take time each day for devotions and prayer. Dedicate yourself to the Lord, and He will make you a leader of men.

3. Be thankful. Try to list one thing you are grateful for each day. At the end of the week, review it. You might be amazed at what God shows you. A thankful heart can also be one that is ready to help. Besides, God has called us to serve others.

These steps will help you depend on the Lord, and doors will open for you to be a support to others.

DAY 28

Keep Your Eyes on the Prize

November 18, 2006: Ohio State 42, Michigan 39

"Let your eyes look straight ahead; fix your gaze directly before you."

—PROVERBS 4:25

The matchup between No. 1 Ohio State against No.2 Michigan was hailed "the game of the century."

Both teams were undefeated and contended for a trip to the BCS National Championship game. For the first time ever, two top-ranked teams in the nation met for a chance to play for the national crown. More than 106,000 fans crammed into the Horseshoe to watch the epic battle between two of college football's legendary schools.

Troy Smith decided to have a spectacular day and wipe away any hopes of an upset from Michigan. The Heisman Trophy winner put the team on his shoulders and carried them to a first half lead. The All-American quarterback zig-zagged and razzle-dazzled all day.

On one occasion, he play-faked a run and found Ted Ginn Jr. open for a 39-yard touchdown strike to give OSU a 21-7 lead. Ohio State had a mere four-point lead with 10 minutes left to play in the game. But Smith put the game away when he found Brian Robiski open for a 13-yard pass for the score.

Smith passed for 316 yards and completed 29 of 41 attempts with four TDs. So much was at stake, and he knew the value of the game. The Buckeyes won the game 42-39 and earned a spot in the national championship.

Afterward, he said, "This is the Ohio State University-Michigan game. It's the biggest game in college football." A chance to play in the championship game was not even on his mind. He could have looked ahead to what was to come. But he focused on the game he had to play at the time. He put aside "what might be" and concentrated on "what is now."

> "You will keep in perfect peace those whose minds are steadfast, because they trust in you."

> —ISAIAH 26:3

Are you focused on Jesus? Or do you try to anticipate the future instead?

4th and 1: Preparation for a family vacation or working to build a retirement account are both good things to do, but don't run ahead of God and attempt to plan the future for yourself. Perhaps you long for a way to serve the Lord, but the doors continue to shut. Have you considered this might be the Lord telling you to wait on His timing?

Goal Line Stand: The best way to stay in stride with Christ is simple, yet people sometimes lose focus. Try these five steps to keep your sights on Him instead of the future:

1. Begin the day with God. Clear out the sleep in your eyes and read a chapter or two from the Bible while you drink your morning coffee. What a wonderful way to stay in tune with what Jesus has in store for you. Or you

might like to read the Word at bedtime. In any case, find time to devote to the scriptures. Start or end your day with the Word of God, a playbook you can't do without.

2. <u>Remain in an attitude of prayer.</u> Communication with your Coach is vital. Stay humble and keep your thoughts on the entire picture God has promised us as His children.

3. <u>Serve the Master.</u> Allocate more time to serve the Lord and others, and you will stay focused on what is important in life.

4. <u>Limit distractions.</u> At times, we become consumed and busy with life, and we lose focus on what God wants us to do. Introduce more discipline into your regular routine and shove out the unnecessary events that can hinder your walk. Turn off the television or shut down social media for the evening and give your attention to your family or a worthy cause.

5. <u>Get rid of the sin.</u> Don't let a few bad habits get in your way. Identify them and kick them out of the game.

Troy Smith did not look ahead to the national title game before OSU took on Michigan. Knock off the enemy you have now. Don't plan for the future so much you get caught off guard. Keep your focus on the task at hand, and serve the Lord today.

DAY 29

Stiff Arm the Devil

September 8, 2007: Ohio State 20, Akron 2

"Do not give the devil a foothold."

—EPHESIANS 4:27

The game between host Ohio State and Akron was not even a fair matchup. The Buckeyes rolled to a 20-2 non-conference win over the Zips.

Tailback Chris "Beanie" Wells rushed for 143 yards on 20 carries, but this is not what earned him the nickname "the arm of harm." He used his power to stiff arm a defender to the ground on one of the runs toward the end zone. The play caught the eyes of the nation.

Who remembers when he shoved a Louisiana State University defender and slung him about five yards away toward the end of a 29-yard run during a national title game? Wells was famous for this power shove and used it to perfection many times throughout his career at Ohio State. In three years as a Buckeye, he gained 3,382 yards on 585 carries with 30 touchdowns. He proved to be a force to be reckoned with, more than ever when he used this tactic.

The move is defined as follows:

A stiff arm is the name of a move a football player does to defend the football (it's always the player who runs with the ball). While he has the ball in one hand, the other arm sticks out and stiffens, hence the name stiff arm. Stronger players can use this technique more effectively.

To be effective at this technique, a player must first be strong. He must also be agile and use power. The move is effective because its force is applied down the length of the straightened arm, right into the shoulders. The force can be applied to topple a defender who approaches. The successful use of the maneuver can render a tackler useless and send him to the ground.

Take note of the Heisman Trophy. The sculpted player is depicted in the famous stiff arm pose prepared to fend off a would-be tackler.

"Submit yourselves, then, to God. Resist the devil, and he will flee from you."

—JAMES 4:7

Are you strong enough to stiff arm Satan?

4th and 1: Perhaps you have a close walk with the Lord. Maybe you teach Sunday school or sing in the choir. You love to use your talents to glorify the King of Kings. All may seem right with the world when from out of nowhere, a blitz comes from the devil. He charges hard at you with accusations from your past. Are you strong enough to avoid the tackle? Can you stiff arm him to the ground and run toward the goal line?

Goal Line Stand: Christians are not strong enough to thwart a tackle from the force of evil alone. We must depend on God to block for us. Here are some tips to strengthen your faith and depend on the Lord to fend off the enemy:

1. Realize you are no match alone. You must submit yourself to God. Do not let pride get in the way. A man who admits his weakness and depends on the Lord is indeed strong.

2. Be confident. God is on your side! The devil lies to us and tries to make us feel we invite the battles on ourselves. But once the Lord forgives your sins, He does not remember them, and moves on. The devil reminds you of your yesterdays, and he tries to convince you that you are not in anyone's good graces, let alone God's. But Christ has thrown your sins into the sea of forgetfulness. Don't go fishing for them.

3. The Lord wins in the end. Read the book of Revelation, and see the box score for yourself. God wins.

4. Praise your way through the attack. Give the devil a stiff arm and raise your arms to give God glory. No defender can touch you when you exercise this maneuver. Use it often.

Wells used the stiff arm to perfection. As a believer, you too can become strong and cast the devil out in Jesus' name.

DAY 30

Make Your Heavenly Reservation

November 22, 1975: Ohio State 21, Michigan 14

"For the Son of Man is going to come in his Father's glory with his angels, and then he will reward each person according to what they have done."

—MATTHEW 16:27

At the time, the game was called one of Ohio State's greatest comebacks. The Buckeyes were outplayed by Michigan most of the game and could not muster a strong offensive attack. The Big House was full of anticipation as the Wolverines appeared primed to knock off their conference rivals.

OSU signal caller Cornelius Greene took matters into his own hands in the final quarter and led the Bucks 80 yards in 11 plays. Pete Johnson plowed his way to the goal line for the score to tie the game at 14.

Johnson, a 250-pound fullback, scored three touchdowns that day for Ohio State.

The score that won the game came with 2:19 to play when he romped into the end zone from three yards out. The win gave the Buckeyes their 11th Big Ten title and their first victory in Ann Arbor in eight years, and they punched their ticket to play in the prestigious Rose Bowl.

"Rejoice and be glad, because great is your reward in heaven, for in the same way they persecuted the prophets who were before you."

—MATTHEW 5:12

Do you long to make a comeback? Have you secured your reservation for Heaven?

4th and 1: Were you once on fire for the Lord? Have you slacked off in your service to the kingdom? Can you do more for Him? Are you still a Christian? These are tough questions to ask. Take inventory of your soul, and the answers can make a difference where you spend eternity. All Christians should adopt a system of checks and balances. Everyday hustle and bustle can distract us at times. If you feel you might be slacking in your walk with Christ, examine your heart. If you no longer read your Bible and fall behind in your church attendance, this might be an indication the enemy has control of your game. Don't give up. You can return and claim your rewards in Heaven.

Goal Line Stand: You must possess the fortitude and determination to stage a resurgence. To pull it off, you need a series of successful play calls along with clutch performances. Follow these steps if you feel you are behind in the game:

1. <u>You must first realize and admit your condition.</u> Do not worry about ego or shame. Your soul is more important than what a nosy neighbor might think. Unfortunately, the game of life has no scoreboard. We must always be the ones who keep track of the score. We can also depend on true friends to tell us when we are behind in the game. Once you grasp you are in trouble, you can

look at God's playbook and launch an attack against Satan to get back into position and score.

2. <u>Return to the Word of God.</u> One of the first signs of a falling away is when you slack off on your devotions. When other priorities take you away from your Bible time and prayer life, you know you have a problem. In the dark of the night, deep down you are aware of your thoughts. Don't be afraid, instead be bold and delve into His Word.

3. <u>Be faithful to attend church.</u> When a player doesn't go to practice, his skills diminish and he is not ready for the next game. A coach might also penalize the player who skips out. The same happens when you don't go to the house of the Lord. Your pastor and those who love you notice too. When you miss services on purpose, you tell Christ He does not matter. Don't duck out and miss the game. You're only hurting yourself.

4. <u>Remove sin from your life.</u> If you are behind in the game, chances are you allowed the devil to hold sin and temptation over you. You know the difference between right and wrong. When in doubt, refrain and ask the Lord to help you. The devil will never tell you to go to church, and he will not instruct you to pray. When you hear a still small voice instruct you to read your Bible, pray, and go to church, rest assured it is from Heaven.

Don't ever think it's too late to make the comeback. Win the game and make your reservation for the largest championship trophy of all—eternity in Heaven.

DAY 31

A God of Second Chances

January 3, 2003: Ohio State 31, Miami 24
2OT National Championship

"Yet this I call to mind and therefore I have hope: Because of the Lord's great love we are not consumed, for his compassions never fail. They are new every morning; great is your faithfulness."

—LAMENTATIONS 3:21-23

The hype that led up to the National Championship game was right on target. The matchup between the No. 2 ranked Ohio State Buckeyes and the No. 1 Miami Hurricanes looked like a college football fan's dream game. Miami entered the showdown the heavy favorite, and had won 34 straight games before they headed to Tempe, Arizona. Most experts predicted Ohio State to be outplayed and defeated.

The game has been hailed as one of the greatest events in the history of college sports. The gridiron battle ended in regulation tied at 17. The Hurricanes scored on their initial drive in the first overtime period. The mission now was to stop Ohio State.

Field general Craig Krenzel dropped back on fourth and three on the Miami five-yard line. His aim was wide receiver Chris Gamble. The ball hit the ground, and the Miami celebration ensued. Fireworks went off, and the team stormed the field. Seconds later, a yellow flag fluttered in the air and landed in the corner of the end zone. A Miami defender was called for pass interference, and the Bucks had another opportunity.

Ohio State made the most of the second chance when Krenzel dove across the goal to send the game into a second OT. After Maurice Clarett soared into the end zone and his team made a dramatic defensive stop, OSU won the title.

Years after the interference call was made, it remains a topic of debate. Miami fans say it should not have been whistled, while Buckeye faithful hold a different opinion. Neither arguments change the fact Ohio State won the game and took home the crown.

The Buckeyes took advantage of the opportunity and adjusted. Miami did not.

> *"Then Peter came to Jesus and asked, 'Lord, how many times shall I forgive my brother or sister who sins against me? Up to seven times?' Jesus answered, 'I tell you, not seven times, but seventy-seven times."*
>
> —MATTHEW 18:21-22

Has the Lord given you a second chance? Do you plan to make the most of it, or will you sit around and complain or stew over circumstances from your past?

4th and 1: Once the Lord gives you another opportunity, you must act and display a positive attitude—make an impact. Forgiveness is a wonderful, miraculous gift. You can entertain two opinions about the play in question. 1) The Hurricanes committed a penalty, or 2) The Bucks were given a second chance. Are you satisfied to sit around and wonder what might have been, or do you have a desire to dive into the end zone and win the game?

Goal Line Stand: God grants forgiveness to you when you ask. The hardest part about this is when you realize you must you let your sin go. Mistakes fester and brew in your mind and memory. Learn from them and go forward. Not once should you let your past get in the way of your future. Don't ever return to the old ways; instead, remember the pain it caused and use it as motivation to be successful. Make it a purpose to score and come out a winner. Here are some tips to win the game in overtime:

1. Forgive others. Just as the Lord has wiped away your sins, you too must let go when people have offended or hurt you.

2. Be thankful. God gave His life for you so you may live in Heaven. Never forget the fact, and realize the sacrifice He suffered and the debt He paid.

3. Stay focused. Let the past go, and develop a plan to usher in honor and glory to His kingdom.

4. Be productive for Christ. Let the Lord steer you in the way He wants you to go. You can help with an active ministry or volunteer for your favorite charity. You might even mail letters or send flowers to be an encouragement to people.

5. Praise Him always. No matter what happens in your day, give the Lord glory. He deserves it from you.

After you do this, you will be better equipped and ready to make the big play when God forgives you. Make the most of your OT period.

DAY 32

Go Deep in the Lord

November 9, 2002: Ohio State 10, Purdue 6

"I pray that the eyes of your heart may be enlightened in order that you may know the hope to which he has called you, the riches of his glorious inheritance in his holy people..."

—EPHESIANS 1:18

The No. 2 ranked Buckeyes had the entire season on the line. They trailed host Purdue with under two minutes left in the game. A perfect record, a Big Ten title, and an appearance in the national title game were in jeopardy.

Jim Tressel was a conservative coach. A fourth and one signaled a run up the gut with Maurice Clarett. Not in this case. Quarterback Craig Krenzel dropped back and connected with receiver Michael Jenkins for a 37-yard touchdown strike with 96 seconds left in the game. The play secured the narrow 10-6 win over Purdue in the conference matchup. Ohio State remained undefeated at 11-0, and its hopes for a national crown stayed alive.

After the game, Krenzel, who passed for 173 on a 9-11 performance, said he wished everyone could experience the natural high he had that night. The deep pass worked for OSU and kept them in the hunt for the ultimate prize. When the opponent did not expect them to, they went deep.

"...and his incomparably great power for us who believe. That power is the same as the mighty strength he exerted when he raised Christ from the dead and seated him at his right hand in the heavenly realms."

—EPHESIANS 1: 19-20

Can you go deeper in your relationship with the Lord?

4th and 1: Have you discovered you might be in a rut? This takes place in the lives of the best of Christians. The journey you are on is lengthy, and you must pace yourself. Too much of anything can lead to burnout. But as a follower of Christ, you must be on guard against this sneaky tool used by the devil. He wants you to do the same thing over and over again until you become complacent. His plan will not allow you to reach your goal to gain, and he will force you to punt away instead of win.

Goal Line Stand: I'm sure you can relate to how the Buckeyes felt on fourth down. If they didn't reach the first down marker, everything they had worked for was gone. You need to gather yourself and make a play. But when you make it to the line, you see a different defense in place. You pray, and the Lord gives you an audible, and you change the play at the line of scrimmage. You go long and connect for the unexpected TD. Then you experience the natural high Krenzel described. However, in this case it's a spiritual high. Here are a few ways to bust off the line and make an impactful play:

1. The Lord may want you to start a ministry. Maybe He wants you to mail cards of encouragement. Or He might want you to witness one-on-one to prisoners in the local jail. We have many ways we can go deep for

Christ, promote His Word, and tell of His wonderful grace. Perhaps you have talent to write or broadcast as a minister. Make the call, and go for the score.

2. The Lord might signal for you to stop an activity. Maybe you are in a situation where Christ directs you to switch gears. Or you are selfish and have the wrong priorities. Your life might be centered on what YOU want, and not what God desires for you. Get in the prayer huddle, and listen to the coach.

3. The Lord may direct you to give more. When you sacrifice with no expectations in return, God honors your actions. You are expected to tithe. But when you go above and beyond to spread the Word, you will be rewarded by Him.

4. The Lord might want you to be more involved. Busy people obtain results. Can you take on more responsibility? Do you want to be blessed by God? Maybe He has signaled you to increase your work for the Kingdom.

5. Perhaps the Lord may want you to give away certain possessions. Maybe you put something ahead of God. Now He instructs you to lay it on the altar of sacrifice and give it away. When you obey the Lord, He will not forget nor forsake. When you demonstrate that He means more to you than any item on earth, then you become of great value to Him.

When you read the Word of God and pray more, you will find yourself in a deeper relationship with Christ. You will connect with the long pass to win the game and remain undefeated by the devil.

DAY 33

Find Your Courage

September 30, 1995: Ohio State 45, Notre Dame 26

"Be strong and courageous. Do not be afraid or terrified because of them, for the Lord your God goes with you; he will never leave you nor forsake you."

—DEUTERONOMY 31:6

Notre Dame had one goal when its players strolled into the Horseshoe—an upset over Ohio State. The two college football powerhouse teams had not faced each other in about 60 years.

The No.15 Fighting Irish made a bold statement and jumped out to a 10-0 lead in the second quarter. Ohio State, ranked No. 7, reached down and countered with two scores. Quarterback Bobby Hoying connected with receiver Terry Glenn for one TD and with Dimitrious Stanley for the second one. The Buckeyes trailed 17-14 at the break.

In the second half, OSU proved why it was a team to be reckoned with as it scored 31 points. Hoying fired for two more scores, one to Buster Tilman and another to Glenn, while ball carrier Eddie George rumbled for 207 yards and two TDs, one which included a 61-yard bolt to seal the win.

The team found the courage at halftime to ruin Notre Dame's aspirations to pull off the unthinkable.

"Have not I commanded you? Be strong and courageous. Do not be afraid; do not be discouraged, for the Lord your God will be with you wherever you go."

—JOSHUA 1:9

Has fear ever darkened your door and caused you to lack courage?

4th and 1: Fear is a natural and human emotion. Some people shiver and agonize at the thought of the unknown. There are many circumstances in life people may not understand. For instance, some may face job loss and wonder how the bills will be paid. Others might have a storm of illness in their lives which poses serious problems. The past might rear its nasty head and make you doubt your salvation. Decisions must be made with courage and boldness.

The Buckeyes went up against a team determined to knock them out of the race for the No. 1 spot. They gathered themselves together at the half and demonstrated courage in a time of uncertainty.

Goal Line Stand: You might have to make an unpopular choice. Deep within your soul, you know it's the right thing to do. But you must depend on the Lord to guide you through difficult times and follow His playbook. Step back, and know Christ is on your side. Consider these suggestions to show more courage:

1. <u>Hold tight to your convictions.</u> The enemy will tell you to "chill out" and "live a little bit." His is not the best advice. If you have a dress code for your children, enforce it. Your co-workers might want you to slip out and take a drink with them when you hold a standard against

such activity. Never compromise, but you can explain. A door may open and present you an opportunity to share the gospel in a sincere manner. You can witness to others, sharing the rules you follow and describe the consequences. But you can only do that if you don't join in with the crowd.

2. <u>Demonstrate faith instead of fear.</u> If you lost your job, show courage and trust the Lord will provide. He might come through at the start of the search for a new position, or He could wait until the last minute. Prepare and look. Do your part to find a replacement, but have faith He will always provide. You or a loved one might run into medical issues and life may get uncertain, but show confidence in His love and mercy for you. This may also require more time in prayer and in the Word of God. You will find comfort while you wait.

3. <u>Do more for those around you.</u> The Lord has called you to show love to those who need help. He encourages you to be bold and show audacity. No matter the circumstances, He expects you to demonstrate His will and be the light to those in darkness. Go the extra mile to help others who are less fortunate. Do what oftentimes takes courage. Remember, all the glory goes to Him, not yourself.

If you find yourself behind in the halftime of life, give yourself a pep talk. Dive into the Scriptures and find the perfect play to allow you to break the game wide open and ensure your victory.

DAY 34

Be Grounded and Avoid Controversy

November 24, 1973: Ohio State 10, Michigan 10

"For I see that you are full of bitterness and captive to sin."

—ACTS 8:23

Both Ohio State and Michigan were undefeated. The Buckeyes were ranked No. 1 while the Wolverines sat at No. 4. Enormous implications for both rode on the outcome of the contest. A conference title, a possible Rose Bowl appearance and a chance at a national championship were up for grabs.

Prior to the game, Ann Arbor, Michigan, was pounded with rain, which meant most of the game would be fought on the turf. Neither team put together effective offensive drives. Ohio State took a 3-0 lead in the second quarter with a field goal by Blair Conway. Just before the half, Ohio State fullback Pete Johnson plowed through for a touchdown and a 10-0 lead.

Michigan clawed its way back in the second half and cut the deficit to 10-3. QB Dennis Franklin later scored a TD when he scampered 10 yards to tie the game at 10-10. The Wolverines had two opportunities to win the game in the final three minutes, but they failed to connect on two missed field goal attempts. At the time, college football rules did not allow for an overtime to be played. Now, who earned the right to go to the Rose Bowl? OSU Coach Woody Hayes did not think his Bucks would be selected, and Michigan had a strong belief they should be tapped.

Two years earlier, the Big Ten had ended the rules which said no team could appear in consecutive Rose Bowls. If this was still in effect, Michigan had a clear-cut choice to go to Pasadena, even if it lost the game.

The next day, athletic directors from the conference tapped Ohio State again to represent the Big Ten at the Grand Daddy of them all.

The vote surprised the Buckeyes and infuriated the Wolverines, who gave partial blame to Michigan State after it voted against them. The Spartan vote was perhaps in retaliation to a previous Wolverine vote to deny the Spartans membership into the conference.

The results of the vote have always been a sore spot for Michigan and Coach Bo Schembechler, who carried his disappointment over the decision all the way to the grave.

There was a lot of speculation about who influenced who in the final decision process. As a result, several rule changes were made by the NCAA, which included an expansion of bowl bids to more teams. Both squads deserved to go to the Rose Bowl, but the Bucks got the nod. The selection left a bitter taste in the mouths of many Michigan loyalists.

> "Get rid of all bitterness, rage and anger, brawling and slander, along with every form of malice. Be kind and compassionate to one another, forgiving each other, just as Christ God forgave you."
>
> —EPHESIANS 4:31-32

Do you harbor emotions like Schembechler? Resentment and bitterness have no place in the life of a Christian.

4th and 1: If you have gone through similar emotions, like we all do from time to time, you must address the issue right off the bat. If you let them sit and fester, they will consume your life and destroy your walk with the Lord.

Goal Line Stand: After you realize bitterness has made its way into your life, you must take action to remove it forever. Here are some suggestions how to tackle the emotions for a win:

1. <u>Find comfort in Scripture.</u> Remember the Lord said He would never leave you. He did not promise an easy life. Depend on the Word of God more and find a verse you can relate to. John 16:33 is a good one. *"I have told you these things, so that in me you may have peace. In this world you will have trouble. But take heart! I have overcome the world."*

2. <u>Forgive.</u> This is not as easy as it sounds, but it remains an essential part of our lives. Even if the person who wronged you has not apologized—forgive anyway. In Psalm 51, the Lord instructs us to keep a pure heart.

3. <u>Throw it out.</u> The best way to dispose of bitterness in your life is to toss out the garbage that causes you to falter. If you don't, the nasty smell of trash will consume you.

4. <u>Praise it away.</u> When you lift your hands in prayer and worship, the devil *must* flee. He does not want any part of you when you give thanks to the Lord. When you have a grateful spirit, forgiveness comes easier, and bitterness will depart.

People let pride control their lives. Don't fall into this condition and let it ruin your witness. Don't let an athletic director decide your fate on a conference call. Instead, beat them to the punch. Get the Lord on the line, and let Him tell you what to do for His glory.

DAY 35

Don't be a Cold Christian

November 5, 1950: Michigan 9, Ohio State 3

"So, because you are lukewarm—neither hot nor cold—I am about to spit you out of my mouth."

—REVELATION 3:16

The Snow Bowl. The game was played in an all-out blizzard, where more than five inches of snow fell on the field in the Horseshoe. To make conditions worse, a gale of 30-mile-per-hour winds blew throughout the contest. About 50,000 brave souls came out to watch the matchup.

A Big Ten Conference Championship and a trip to the Rose Bowl hung on the frozen line. Conditions made it tough to play the contest. The wind and snow made it hard for players to run or pass. For the fans, it brought misery. For the players, it was torture.

The strategy of each team was the same. Run the pigskin straight through the middle, hope to gain some ground and try for a field goal. Most of the time, the attempts were made on third down in case frozen fingers fumbled the ball.

Michigan won the game 9-3.

"For I know the plans I have for you,' declares the Lord, 'plans to prosper you and not harm you, plans to give you hope and a future."

—JEREMIAH 29:11

Are you lukewarm or cold when it comes to the service of the Lord?

4th and 1: Have you cut back on the time you spend in God's Word? Have you reduced your fellowship with other believers? Do you look and dress comparable to the world? Do you admire Hollywood actors and read about their lives more than those in scripture? Is your taste in music more and more secular? Do you take a glance at social media or the internet while you read the Bible? Do you hesitate to talk to others about Christ? Have your convictions changed? Has your relationship with the Lord been damaged? These are tough questions to ask yourself, but they are necessary when you suspect your walk with God has become frigid. If you are not careful, you will find yourself in a spiritual Snow Bowl. When Michigan and Ohio State played the game, everyone was miserable and just wanted it to be over.

Goal Line Stand: Once you realize you demonstrate a cold or frozen complacency toward Jesus and the church, you must begin to thaw. Break the ice and encircle around a fire. Here are ways you can light the match:

1. Read more of the Word of God. You may not have a desire to open the Bible, but you must get warm in order to thaw. Start out slow. Read familiar passages and bring the warmth of Christ into your heart.

2. Pray down fire from heaven. After you read, pray and ask God to administer His Word to your life.

3. Find an enthusiastic church or attend a revival. If you don't stoke fires, they will go out. The same applies to us in our spiritual lives. If you are not in a rejuvenated

church that see souls saved and preaches the truth, go find one.

4. <u>Snuggle up to the fire.</u> Become involved in a ministry or go on a mission trip. You must actively work to ignite a fire in your spirit. Once you do, the heat will rise and your testimony will too.

5. <u>Spread the flames.</u> Challenge yourself to speak more to others about the goodness of the Lord. Fight fire with fire. When you talk to people about Christ, it strengthens you and your witness.

No one likes to spend time with a lukewarm or cold person. A camp fire is much more fun to be around compared to a frozen pond. You can toast s'mores, roast hot dogs, and sing around a fire pit. If you stroll out on a frozen pond, it could crack and you might slide into the frosty waters. Fan the flames and melt the ice that engulfs your heart.

DAY 36

Make Up for Your Mistakes

November 21, 1998: Ohio State 31, Michigan 16

"In him we have redemption through his blood, the forgiveness of sins, in accordance with the riches of God's grace;"

—EPHESIANS 1:7

The lone great accomplishment worthy of notoriety for any Ohio State football coach is to beat the team up north— all the time. Should OSU go 0-9 in the season and defeat Michigan in the end, the year is successful.

John Cooper's record at Ohio State stood at 111-43-4. This is an impressive line for any head coach. However, he was 2-10-1 against the Wolverines—not acceptable for OSU fans. Cooper's last home game came against Michigan. He wanted to go out a winner and redeem himself. His team gave him such an opportunity when it thumped UofM 31-16.

Ohio State set the tone at the start and scored 14 points in the first quarter. The Bucks took a 21-10 lead into the half after QB Joe Germaine connected with David Boston for the score. OSU poured it on in the second half to make sure they sent their leader out on a wonderful note.

Every memory of those lousy years disappeared. In the blink of an eye, he was loved again, even by the fans who always criticized him when he lost "THE GAME" each year.

Do you seek forgiveness?

> *"When these things begin to take place, stand up and lift up your heads, because your redemption is drawing near."*

—LUKE 21:28

4th and 1: Everyone makes mistakes, but not everyone asks for forgiveness. Have you done something, either intentional or not, and wished for forgiveness? In order to obtain it, you need to request to be forgiven. You must realize your error and vow not to make it again. After that, you will be able to take advantage of an opportunity to make good on your gaffe.

Goal Line Stand: No perfect person has ever lived on earth except for Christ. We all mess up and will continue to make mistakes. The key to redemption is to commit to learn from them and to pledge not to repeat them under any circumstances. No one wants to make a blunder, but it does happen. People get hurt and hold grudges. If you have made a poor judgement, consider these suggestions and choose the path of forgiveness:

1. Examine yourself. At times, you might be the last one to realize you have done wrong. Analyze the situation and look into your heart and emotions. You know right from wrong. Never let pride be an obstacle to correct a discrepancy. Let bitterness take a back seat, and be the one who admits when you are out of line.

2. Seek the face of God. Once you take responsibility for your actions, you can approach your Heavenly Father and beg for His forgiveness first. Confession to the Lord is hard, but you feel so much better once you have

completed the task. Ask God for direction and always thank Him for being there for you.

3. <u>Now forgive yourself.</u> Once Christ has forgiven, you must do the same for yourself. When you allow God to show mercy on you, it means you are given a do-over. Take advantage of it and rebuke the devil. Satan will be the one who reminds you of what you once did. Accept the Lord's forgiveness and move on to the next play.

4. <u>Ask for another chance.</u> Pride cannot enter here and must leave. Demonstrate humility at all times. When you show honest remorse to those you wronged, it will go a long way in the forgiveness process. Always accept responsibility, and don't make excuses. If the other person chooses not to let it go, you are off the hook. You are not responsible for how they respond. You have followed and obeyed God's Word.

5. <u>Make up.</u> Find any means to make right what has happened. Time will be a good friend to you at this point. You must earn trust and portray a willingness to sacrifice. It took Coach Cooper 12 years to win over the hearts of the Scarlet and Gray before his departure.

Take the necessary initiatives to make your current impression a positive one. Always leave on a high note. There doesn't have to be a final farewell or a curtain call, like Coach Cooper had, but strive to make a wonderful impact every day of your life. Now you can experience the grace of redemption from the Lord wherever you go.

DAY 37

God Will Deliver in Such a Time

January 1, 1997: Ohio State 20, Arizona State 17

"No, in all these things we are more than conquerors through him who loved us."

—ROMANS 8:37

A movie script could not have done it better.

Ohio State's Joe Germaine grew up in Mesa, Arizona, but he was never offered a scholarship to play at Arizona State University. For the ultimate irony, he led the Buckeyes to a magnificent come-from-behind 20-17 win over the Sun Devils in the prestigious Rose Bowl in Pasadena, California. Germaine was named the MVP. After the game, he said he had a glorious new vision of what victory meant to him. "The way we did it makes it even sweeter," he added.

The No. 2 ranked Arizona State took the lead when Jake Plummer scampered into the end zone for a 17-14 lead with 1:40 to go in the contest. Germaine got the job done after he put together a 65-yard drive with about 90 seconds left on the clock. He connected on several passes throughout the march and culminated with a nine-yard touchdown strike to David Boston with 19 seconds to play. Ohio State held on for the win. Germaine tasted sweet victory and showed the Sun Devils they should not have snubbed him years earlier.

Ohio State finished ranked No. 2, while Arizona's hopes of national championship faded in the sun.

Have you fought a battle and God led you to victory in the end?

> *"But thanks be to God, who always leads us in Christ's triumphal procession and uses us to spread the aroma of the knowledge of him everywhere."*

> —2 CORINTHIANS 2:14

4th and 1: Perhaps you are in a struggle, and the enemy has the lead. What can you do to stage a comeback and win the game? Joe Germaine had personal motivation for the way he played. He wanted to earn the title for the Buckeyes and show ASU they should have given him a chance.

Goal Line Stand: You realize there isn't much time left on the game clock. Tick, tick, tick is the only sound you hear. Orchestrate a come-from-behind drive to be victorious. Confidence must take over. According to the Bible, God wins in the end, right? Take these steps and march toward the goal line:

1. <u>Understand the way the enemy operates.</u> Satan does not play fair. He will throw darts at you from every direction, and he does not care who he hurts. Study the playbook, the Word of God, and stay in tune with your devotions each day.

2. <u>Be active in your walk.</u> Joe Germaine was all over the place in the final drive. He scrambled and made several completions before he made the pass to win the game. Be sure of the signals Christ sends you throughout the game. There are false prophets who will attempt to dis-

tract you. Be in tune with the Holy Spirit, and call an audible at the line of scrimmage.

3. <u>Thwart the devil.</u> When the enemy comes at you with a blitz, hit the tight end on a quick slant. This is the best defense and allows you to keep the drive alive. Reach the goal to gain this advantage. Stay in the Word, and attend church on a regular basis. Seek the Lord in prayer. When you notice the blitz, call out to Christ. He will slant across the middle with His hands open ready to receive your pass.

4. <u>Praise Him in victory.</u> Lift your hands after each win and give Him the glory. The enemy hates this, and he will leave you alone for a bit. He will try to stage a resurgence of his own, but you must take a strong goal line stand and stop him short of the end zone. When you give the Lord credit for the win, you will always be victorious.

Joe Germaine wanted to prove something. He wished to win for the Bucks, but a part of him also wanted to show Arizona State they made a mistake when they did not choose him. Be thankful you are always welcome on God's team, and He will make sure you are in position to win the title. Obey what He says.

DAY 38

You Can Defend Yourself

January 1, 1987: Ohio State 28, Texas A&M 12

"For the one in authority is God's servant for your good. But if you do wrong, be afraid, for rulers do not bear the sword for no reason. They are God's servants, agents of wrath to bring punishment on the wrong doer."

—ROMANS 13:4

Surprises are fun to enjoy on birthdays, Christmas, and other special occasions. This was not the case for Texas A&M on New Year's Day. Ohio State stunned the Aggies 28-12 to win the Cotton Bowl.

The Buckeyes came off a regular season loss to Michigan and wanted to spark things up a little bit. Coach Earl Bruce updated his image from stoic to fashion icon as he donned a suit and fedora straight out of the gangster days of the 1920s. His Bucks wore bright red-hot shoes that could not be ignored. Bruce said after the game he wanted the team to be more flamboyant. The bold look got the attention of everyone.

All-American linebacker Chris Spielman had one of the best days of his career. His interception and return for a touchdown in the third quarter gave the Buckeyes a 14-6 lead. The play also started an onslaught for the OSU defense, as it tormented Aggies QB Kevin Murray, who was picked off five times in the second half.

Spielman dropped back from the linebacker position and grabbed the pass intended for the tight end. He rumbled 24 yards for the first TD of his college career and was the unanimous selection for the outstanding defensive player of the game.

Michael Key put the game away for good for OSU when he intercepted an Aggie pass and returned it for the score with 2:48 to play in the game.

> *"[The people of Judah] who were building the wall. Those who carried materials did their work with one hand and held a weapon in the other, and each of the builders wore his sword at his side as he worked. But the man who sounded the trumpet stayed with me."*

—NEHEMIAH 4:17-18

Can believers in Jesus defend themselves when threatened?

4th and 1: Have you ever been in a situation where you were in danger and, as a child of God, did not take action? Someone might try to take advantage of your beliefs and not expect you to respond. Some think Christians should allow people walk over them and turn the other cheek.

Goal Line Stand: Keep in mind there are people who cannot defend themselves. This might include elderly people or unborn children. It is not the Christian way to allow others to prey on innocent victims. The Lord instructs you to defend those who cannot fend for themselves. You will give an account to Christ on Judgement Day. What can you do as a follower of the Gospel?

1. <u>Respect the law.</u> Hold police officers and first responders up in prayer and thank them for their service. When you honor those who serve you, you honor the Lord. He has placed people before you for protection from evil. Respect and help them.

2. <u>Be aware of what is going on around you.</u> Protect your home and family. Install several outdoor lights or a security system. If God has blessed you with resources, take measures to protect them.

3. <u>Be active.</u> If you are concerned about social issues like euthanasia or abortion, then get involved. There are many pro-life organizations and pregnancy centers who will welcome volunteers. Allow God to bless you, and speak for those who cannot speak for themselves.

4. <u>Know your rights.</u> If your state allows you to carry a concealed firearm, make this a consideration. In today's era of rampant violence, one alternative is to arm yourself with a weapon. Do it within the law and be proactive. Get educated, and pray about it before you decide.

Criminals do not have the right to take advantage of you just because you are a child of God. There is a time and place to be righteous. Defend your life and property, and claim the protection of the Lord. He doesn't expect you to be a vigilante, nor does He expect you to be a victim.

DAY 39

God's Timing is Best

November 17, 1984: Ohio State 21, Michigan 6

"For the revelation awaits an appointed time; it speaks of the end and will not prove false. Though it linger, wait for it; it will certainly come and will not delay."

—HABAKKUK 2: 3

The Buckeyes had waited five years since their last appearance in the Rose Bowl. To most fans, it was an eternity.

Head Coach Earl Bruce decided to toss out the spread formation and return to the traditional Power I formation. And why not? He had mighty Keith Byars in the backfield. Byars made all three touchdowns and almost surpassed a record set by legend Archie Griffin. Before the game, he needed 142 yards to break Griffin's conference season rushing record of 1,695 yards in one year. He finished the day with 113 yards on 28 totes, just shy by 29 yards.

Byars was excited after the game. In one day, the team defeated Michigan, won the Big Ten championship, and secured a spot in the Rose Bowl against Southern Cal. Christmas came for him in November.

The win was not apparent until the fourth quarter when OSU protected a 7-6 lead. Bruce called a play which sent Byars into the end zone from two yards out. He later scored again to put the game away with 4:43 to go in the contest.

Fans who wore the Scarlet and Gray were nervous throughout the game, but they were able to breathe easier when Byars plunged in toward the end.

Michigan Coach Bo Schembechler said OSU played well, but his squad gave it away with too many penalties and turnovers.

> *"He has made everything beautiful in its time. He has also set eternity in the human heart; yet no one can fathom what God has done from beginning to end."*
>
> —ECCLESIASTES 3:11

Have you ever waited on the Lord?

4th and 1: You hope God will show up at the right time. A predicament might be avoided if He reveals Himself and saves the day. You are nervous, just like the Buckeye faithful toward the end of the game. You are encouraged but need a sign the situation will be okay. Do you long for something to be done for you? Will you wait on the Lord? Why does He make us wait?

Goal Line Stand: Perhaps the Lord wants to teach you a lesson and show you a fantastic revelation of great importance to you. No one likes to wait. For instance, we live in a drive-through society and demand results—now. In order to wait on the Lord, consider these recommendations:

1. God instructs you to be patient. Demonstrate patience in a small situation, and this will assist you in the larger problems of life. No matter the size of the issue, trust God with all your heart and accept His answers when He says yes, or no. You are anxious to hear about a job

interview today. But the Lord will inform you when it's appropriate. Should you miss out on a possible job, consider God may have other plans for you.

2. Build character while you wait. Increase your prayer life in times of anticipation. Focus your energy to praise and thank Him during this trial. God uses this time to draw you closer to Him and teach you valuable lessons about how to depend on His timing and His plan. His way is always best. Don't get ahead of Him, and don't get in His way. Stand still and wait on God to move in your situation, and listen for His instructions.

3. Praise the Lord all the time. There is always time to give glory to Christ. Be content in whatever situation you find yourself, no matter the obstacles.

4. Turn your worry over to the Lord. Do not fret about the future. God is in control, and He expects you to trust Him. Instead shift your time and attention to your church or to a charity. When you work in the name of the Lord, rest assured you will receive the whole nine yards.

You might be in a tight game. Go to your playbook—the Bible—and read the last play. It is found in the book of Revelation. In fact, read the entire portion. You will be encouraged and reminded of who wins in the end.

DAY 40

Lead Your Own Script O-H-I-O

"If it is to encourage, then give encouragement; if it is giving, then give generously; if it is to lead, do it diligently; if it is to show mercy, do it cheerfully."

—ROMANS 12:8

The Ohio State Marching Band opens each home game at the historic Horseshoe with one of the most iconic traditions in college football—the performance of Script Ohio by all 192 members of the band. This fan-favorite event generates excitement and prepares the crowd to cheer on the Buckeyes.

The first Script Ohio was performed by OSU's biggest rival. The University of Michigan's band stomped out Ohio in a game in 1932, according to records at the OSU archives, which is ironic. Ohio State first performed it at a 1936 game against Indiana. At the time, there were about 120 members.

Today this heralded tradition culminates with the ultimate honor bestowed on a senior sousaphone player— AKA tuba player. When the lone senior high steps his way to "dot the I" in Ohio, the crowd goes crazy in support of the timeless masterpiece.

To execute the entire Script Ohio, the whole band must follow one person—the drum major. This leader is decked out in a stylish uniform and carries a huge baton. If he gets out of line, then the whole shebang becomes a mess.

Script Ohio is an awesome spectacle and sends chills down the backs of those who observe the tradition.

> *"When the Lord takes pleasure in anyone's way, he causes their enemies to make peace with them."*

> —PROVERBS 16:7

Are you a follower or a leader? The world needs both. But God has called you to be an innovator. He doesn't want you to stay on the sidelines. He depends on you to set a high moral and biblical standard in your home.

Follow the Drum Major: You might find yourself in a position at work where you are obligated to take charge of a project. Or maybe you long to strengthen your relationship with your children. Kids today crave leadership and look for a spiritual example who will be a beacon to them. You can feel alone at times when you lead, because it's not always easy. But the rewards can be worth it when you see the end results. Assume your role and demonstrate why you can be the one who leads a home or manages a project. Confidence and humility must go hand in hand.

Dot the "I": Most men are born with a deep desire to be a leader. Some take leadership for granted, while others may abuse the opportunity. To be an effective leader, you must carry a large baton the same way the Drum Major does for the Buckeyes. At home, our baton is the Word of God. Follow these suggestions, and your family band will be right behind you, step by step. The same goes for a single mother, who

strives alone at times, determined in her heart to provide for
her children:

1. <u>Go to church together.</u> You are the parent. If there is any
   dissension, take control of the situation and enforce the
   rules. Attend the house of the Lord together, and you
   will draw closer to each other.

2. <u>Pray as a team.</u> Let your children know you love them.
   Pray as a family, letting each person take their turn.
   Hold hands and lift their names up to the Lord.

3. <u>Treat your spouse with respect.</u> When your children
   observe you treat your spouse with honor and love, they
   will admire you.

4. <u>Become involved with church or school activities.</u> Don't
   play favorites, always include everyone. Follow the rules,
   show sportsmanship, and honor the U.S. flag.

5. <u>Show sacrifice.</u> When your children perceive you give
   more of yourself than you take, this will resonate, and
   you will reap rewards later.

You don't have to scream and shout to be an effective leader.
You may have times when you must be stern and enforce rules
and curfews to adjust an attitude. But be strong, and above
all, let the love of God shine through you. A successful leader
recognizes when to pull and when to push. You, too, can have
a wonderful tradition similar to Script Ohio in your home.
Let your family witness you spell out C-H-R-I-S-T in your
walk each day.

ABOUT THE AUTHOR

Del Duduit is an award-winning writer and a life-long resident of Southern Ohio. As a sports writer, he has won awards from the Associated Press, the Ohio Prep Sports Writers Association, and the Ohio News Network.

As a Christian writer, he earned the Outstanding Author award at the 2017 Ohio Christian Writers Conference, as well as two other first place awards.

His articles have been published in *Clubhouse Magazine, Sports Spectrum, Bridges,* and *PM Magazine.* He is a co-editor and writer for *Southern Ohio Christian Voice* (sohiochristianvoice.com), and his articles have also been published on *One Christian Voice, Toddstarnes.com, The Sports Column* and *Almost-An-Author.* His weekly blog, *My New Chapter,* appears on *delduduit.com,* and he is a contributing writer for Athletes in Action and *The Christian View Online Magazine.* He is represented by Cyle Young of Hartline Literary Agency.

Del and his wife, Angie, are the parents of two adult sons, Gabe and Eli. They attend Rubyville Community Church.

CPSIA information can be obtained
at www.ICGtesting.com
Printed in the USA
BVHW031412221219
567504BV00001B/144/P